The Usual Suspects Presents
Amazing Facts & Crazy Quizzes
Bullies, Bears and other Bothersome Behaviors

Written by David D. Dye Sr.

Illustrations by Jon Dye

No part of this publication may be reproduced, stored in a retrieval system, or transmitted in any form or by any means, electronic, mechanical, photocopying, recording, or otherwise, without written permission of the publisher.
For information regarding permission, write to
Monarch Publishing Group
Attention: Permissions Department
P. O. Box 2154
Mansfield, TX 76063

ISBN 978-0692621059

Library of Congress Control Number: 2016930901

Text copyright © 2016 by David D. Dye Sr.
Illustrations copyright © 2016 by Jon Dye

Printed in the U.S.A.

Changing Our Small World...One Good Book at a Time™

Dedicated to those who understand that teaching must
be done from the "inside-out" to train the whole person.

A portion of the proceeds from the sale of this book
will be donated to Manna Worldwide which is a non-profit
organization set on "Rescuing children from the grip of poverty".

I would like to thank my friends, family, and coworkers
for their support and willingness to edit, evaluate and
evolve my concepts of the Usual Suspects.
D.D.

Table of Contents

Why You Need this Book	Page i
The Benefits	Page ii
About Bullying and the Usual Suspects	Page iii
How to Use this Book	Page vi
Tips for Student Readers	Page vii
Meet the Usual Suspects	Page viii
TALK-WALK-TELL	Page xv
Amazing Facts and Crazy Quizzes	Page 1
References	Page 115
Other Books by the Author	Page 119

Why You Need this Book

"Give a man a fish and you feed him for a day;
Teach a man to fish and you feed him for a lifetime[1]."

- Ancient Chinese proverb

The goal of a school counselor should be to offer a proactive program that teaches students and staff to fish. As the ancient proverb suggests, helping others has a limited benefit, while training them to deal with their own needs provides a long-term solution. When we teach a student to handle aggressive social interactions on their own, it will potentially solve the problem today, tomorrow, and a lifetime.

The Amazing Facts and Crazy Quizzes is part of the professional educator's fishing kit. It is not the whole kit, but it just might be the hook, line, and sinker as it constantly reminds students and staff how to deal with bullying and other bothersome behaviors. The daily commentary deals with real world experiences and research based solutions. In addition, it touches the hot issues that students deal with every day.

The American School Counselor's Association's National Model emphasizes that school counselors maximize student growth by addressing areas such as respect for self and others, developing positive relationships, resolving conflict, personal safety, and survival skills[2]. In addition, school counselors address self-confidence development, decision-making, problem-solving skills, interpersonal effectiveness, social skills, communication skills, and responsible behavior[3]. Amazing Facts and Crazy Quizzes teach, reteach and reiterate these essentials to the school community on a daily basis.

1. Tripp, 1970,
2. Paone, Lepkowski, 2007,
3. Ockerman, Mason, Hollenbeck, 2012

The Benefits of Using this Tool

- Key issues such as survival skills, conflict resolution, and assertiveness are addressed.

- Personal growth, self-esteem, self-respect, and personal responsibility are promoted.

- Important issues are kept at the forefront of the students' minds with a daily dialogue.

- Bullying strategies are referenced to assist in meeting District and State requirements.

- Provides an opportunity for students and staff to participate in daily announcements.

- It expands the counselor's presence as others can read daily announcements.

- Provides a strong support system if The Usual Suspects or TALK-WALK-TELL is taught through guidance lessons.

- Equips students and staff with knowledge of the Usual Suspect and TALK-WALK-TELL if these are not part of the scheduled guidance lessons.

- Research concludes that when students know the definition of bullying and are exposed to it being used correctly, reported significantly less bullying behavior.

About Bullying and the Usual Suspects

Bullying is well defined, and has had a workable, real world definition for decades. Comparing the work of "bully" experts Dr. Dan Olweus[1], Allan L. Beane[2], and Ken Rigby[3] with the definitions of organizations like the National Education Association[4], and the U.S. Department of Health & Human Services[5], the author has penned the following as an inclusive definition of bullying.

> "Bullying is an intentional, repeated action involving unwanted aggression that is meant to do harm, targeted toward an individual as a result of a real or perceived imbalance of power."

To simplify the definition and make the application user friendly (especially for youth) this definition was adapted into the Five Rules of Bullying. 1) Bullies target their victims[4]. 2) Bullying is a constant (reoccurring) problem[7]. 3) Bullying involves an imbalance of power in favor of the one bullying[1]. 4) Bullying is unwanted aggression[5] and meant to do harm[4]. 5) Bullying is not an accident; it is intentional[8].

During the course of being an educator and school counselor, the author developed an important conclusion about bullying. While a definition had been available for decades, it became obvious during interactions with educators, students, and parents that the definition was either ignored or unknown. It was also observed by the author that while bullying had become a national news topic the definition was being disregarded by media, politicians and professional educators. It appeared that every negative or aggressive social interaction was being reported as bullying, even when the behavior did not meet the most basic components: being intentional, repeated and having an imbalance of power[5]. The author determined to allow the definition to guide the investigations and determine the outcome. In this way, the definition defined the need. Using the five rules of bullying made the process precise, and stress-free.

When the author applied the rules of bullying to the various behaviors being dubbed bullying in his school, many of the cases did not fit the rules. After carefully scrutinizing the real world case studies provided by the students in his academic-community, the need for the Usual Suspects became apparent. If it is not bullying, what is it called? If it is referred to in generic terms (e.g. bully-like behaviors), how can it be properly addressed? With the classification of the Usual Suspects, the author was able to identify bullying and the other behaviors properly and use this knowledge to educate and rehabilitate students who were once treated like malicious bullies.

Allowing the need to design the Suspects

Each character or persona of the Usual Suspects is based on the characteristics of different students observed and served by the author. These similar traits were observed over a course of seven years, in various grade levels and with multiple ethnic and cultural backgrounds. The basis for each of the suspects was gleaned from observation and interaction with individuals with a history of aggressive or abusive home environments, low social skills, physical awkwardness, immaturity, deficient academic skills, and overly stimulated competitive focuses. The researched-based characteristics of those who bully[7], those who are perpetual victims[8], and those who appear bully-proof were also used in the development of additional models.

As a result, the following characters were determined: The Badger, Bear, Bigfoot, Bingo, Buck, Bully, Victor, and Victim. Each persona was developed into a male and female counterpart. On the surface, each of the Negative Social Interactions looked similar to the defined traits of bullying. However, each character lacked one or more parts of the definition. In other words, they did not fit the rules of bullying. The similarities between these suspects and the defined bullying behaviors usually related to the physical interaction. The differences related to motivation, emotions, and methods. For example, the person acting like a Badger may physically poke, push and pull on the target, but the reason for the interaction is the Badger wants to be, or thinks he or she is, the target's friend. This suspect lacks the social skills to have a positive relationship. Instead of treating the student as an aggressor, the student is taught interpersonal skills.

Amazing Facts and Crazy Quizzes is a powerful and proactive way of teaching correct bully information to students and staff with the clarifying characters of the Usual Suspects. To learn more about the Usual Suspects, download the free app, *The Usual Suspects ID Cards* for iPad, Android Tablets and Android smart phones.

1. Olweus, Mortimore, 1993
2. Beane, 2014
3. Rigby, 2007
4. NEA, How to Identify Bullying, 2015
5. Stopbullying.gov | Definition, 2014
6. Olweus, Mortimer, 1993,
7. Dake, Price, Telljohaun, 2003
8. Fagan, Mazerolle, 2011

The Five Rules of Bullying

- Bullies target their victims[1]
- Bullying is not an accident; it is intentional[2]
- Bullying is a constant (reoccurring) problem[3]
- Bullying involves an imbalance of power in favor of the bully[4]
- Bullying is unwanted aggression[5] and meant to do harm[5]

1. NEA, How to Identify Bullying, 2015
2. Fagan, Mazerolle, 2011
3. Dake, Price, Telljohaun, 2003
4. Olweus, Mortimore, 1993
5. Beane, Facts about Bullying, 2014

How to Use this Book

- One hundred and eighty days' worth of amazing facts makes it just right for school announcements

- Appropriate for public, private and parochial school use

- Suitable as a daily discussion-started for the classroom, club or for before and after-school childcare

- Appropriate for Girls and Boys Club, YMCA, city recreation centers and other student-centered programs and organizations

- Just right for parents to bully-proof their children during family devotions or family meetings

- Educators, parents, politicians and other professionals such as counselors, social workers, daycare providers and organizations could use the simple format to learn about the Negative Social Interactions that they are sure to encounter during their duties

- Religious and community leaders could help their audiences understand these serious social concerns.

- Great as a resource for PTA, school, and teacher newsletters

- The up-to-date references provide a library of research material for personal and academic study

- The quick reference guide to the Usual Suspects could be used to help school administrators and other leaders investigate the behavior behind student and workplace incidents

- Written mostly on a 4th grade reading level, Student Readers to be used during presentations of the Amazing Facts and Crazy Quizzes for both elementary and upper grades

Tips for Student Readers

- Stand confident and speak loud and clear. You are sharing important information! Make sure your audience understands you

- Read the text beforehand and make sure you can pronounce each word correctly. Ask for help if you come across a difficult word.

- If you want to be the very best spokesperson, ask someone you trust to listen to you read and ask them if they understand you.

- Respect the punctuation. Periods (.) are like a stop sign. Make a short break or take a breath at the period. Keeping the sentences separated by a short break helps keep the meaning clear.

- The superscript numbers that look like this[1] refer to the references at the bottom of the page. These numbers[1] should not be read.

- Do not say the word (Pause) in a parenthesis. It is a direction for you to give a short break to let the audience think before you continue.

- When you come to the word (repeat) in parenthesis do not read the word (repeat) out loud. This is instructions to you to re-read a sentence or thought.

- Changing the pitch or tone of your voice makes it easier to listen to your reading. Ask a sponsor or perhaps your music teacher to help you with this.

- This is how to read a web address: www.stopbulling.gov/kid is spoken w-w-w Stop-bullying (dot) gov (forward slash) kid.

- As you read a Crazy Quiz, make sure to say the letters for each choice. A) = A. B) = B. This will help the listener stay on track.

- When you come across ____, call them "blank." Example: Bullies ____ (blank) their victims.

- Please do not read the references at the bottom of the page.

Bully Boy / Buhle Belle

Bullying is the trademark of Negative Social Interactions. It can range from the irritating to the downright dangerous. While the social aspect of it has been well defined for decades, the simple rules that define the behavior have been lost in the hustle and bustle of life. Bully Boy and his female counterpart Buhle Belle provide an easy way to teach the specific, research-based, characteristics of bullying.

☑ **Bully Boy and Buhle Belle target their victims**. They are not mean to everyone. They thrive on easy targets and often treat others in a neutral or more positive way. This is why they are hard to catch. (See the Bear)

☑ **Bullying is not an accident; it is on purpose.** Bully Boy and Buhle Belle seek out a victim and targets that person intentionally.

☑ **Bullying is a constant problem.** It occurs every day. When the target sees their Bully coming, they wonder, what will he (or she) do to me this time?

☑ **Bully Boy and Buhle Belle think they have an imbalance of power over the target.** They look for an easy target that they can control physically or emotionally.

☑ **The Bully's actions are unwanted and meant to do harm.** It is not part of a game or group activity. It is not joking around between friends. The Bully is intentionally causing harm.

■ Bully Boy and Buhle Belle meet **FIVE out of the FIVE** rules for bullying.

Buster Bear / Baddie Bear

It is a myth that you can spot a bully from a mile away. Bullying is an action between two individuals. It is not a facial expression or a certain body language. However, as one understands the world of the Usual Suspects he or she realizes that there are other attitudes which provide physical cues. Acting like Buster or Baddie Bear is one such behavior. While bullying is realized through an action, being a bear begins with the attitude. The confusion about Negative Social Interactions happens because there is no distinction made between the bear and bully.

☒ **Buster and Baddie Bear are potentially hostile to anyone.** They think the world is out to "get" them, so he or she plans to "get" them first.

☑ ☒ **Aggression is not an accident, but neither is it planned.** For the slightest reason, Buster or Baddie will retaliate and/or perceive aggression in most accidents.

☑ ☒ **The Bears are a constant problem,** but not to the same person. Their attitudes are a ticking time bomb ready to explode and conducive to violence.

☒ **The Bear doesn't care about an imbalance of power over his target.**
He or she is irrational and may even attack adults.

☑ **Buster's actions are unwanted and meant to do harm.** Bullies try to control targets, but Bear will try to physically hurt his prey.

■ Buster and Baddie Bear meet only **THREE out of the FIVE** rules for bullying.

Billy Badger / Becca Badger

Not every bothersome or rude interaction is bullying. Until the Usual Suspects, the "bully-like" behaviors were undefined and mostly un-addressed. Meet Billy and Becca Badger that represent a behavior that may appear to be bullying because of the physical similarities. Billy Badger may seem to be picking on a person, but he is really trying to be a friend. Key social skills are missing such as empathy, recognizing social cues, understanding personal space and so forth that make Billy and Becca look like bullies in action. Motivation and intent are the key elements in this behavior.

☑ **Billy Badger carefully picks his targets.** He is looking for an individual with whom he feels comfortable enough to interact.

☑ **Badgering is not an accident.** His actions are intentional, but are impulsive, rather than planned.

☑ **Badger might be a constant bother.** As long as he is allowed, he will "pick at" his target.

☒ **He is not trying to overpower his victim.** He is trying to feel like an equal.

☒ **Billy Badger's actions are unwanted and are often misinterpreted.** He does not mean to be mean; he wants to be their friend.

■ Billy and Becca Badger meet only
THREE out of the FIVE rules for bullying.

Bucky Buck / Buckette

There are some kids who like to play rough! Whether they learned watching pro-wrestling, reenacting sports on TV or play-fighting (roughhousing) with dad on Saturday afternoons, Bucky and Buckette associate physical contact with wholesome fun and relationships. It might be a robust attitude toward sports or competition in general. In their mind, the eye is on the prize and how you get there does not matter. As a result, the Bucks wrestle peers to the ground, play-punch kids in the stomach and trash talk their way across the playground.

☒ **Bucky and Buckette are not picky about their targets.** They are just trying to have fun their favorite way: play-fighting, wrestling and roughhousing with anyone close enough to tackle.

☑ **Buck's negative social interaction is not an accident.** His bouts are intentional, but the place and the person involved may be spontaneous.

☑ **The Bucks can be a constant bother.** As long as they are allowed, they will "play rough" with peers.

☒ **Bucky and Buckette do not think in terms of an imbalance of power.** They think everyone wants to rumble: big, small, girl or boy.

☒ **The Buck's actions are unwanted.** They do not intend to hurt; but "no pain no gain" is the competitor's rule. A black eye, scrapes and bruises are all part of the fun.

■ Bucky and Buckette meet only **TWO out of the FIVE rules for bullying.**

Bernie Bigfoot / Bertha Bigfoot

Bernie and Bertha could be called accidental bullies. They do not mean to knock books out of student's hands, run over their classmates in the hall, or demolish the cafeteria in a single bound. They are growing too fast for their coordination and their heads are often too full of fun thoughts to be paying attention to where they are going. The end result may look like bullying, but with a closer look, it is a different matter. The Bigfoots should be taught appropriate skills and should still pay appropriate consequences for their actions.

☒ **Bernie and Bertha Bigfoot do not target their victims.** They are too busy daydreaming to plan an attack.

☑ **Bigfoot might be a constant bother.** As long as they haphazardly roam about without paying attention.

☒ **An Imbalance of power is not involved in these interactions.** Bernie and Becky are a potential nuisance to everyone and anything.

☒ **Bernie and Becky's actions are unwanted, but without an intent to do harm.** He and she do not intend to plow over peers. He and she are impulsive, uncoordinated and do not pay attention.

☒ **Bigfoot blunders are totally by accident.** Accidents are seldom caused by accident. Bernie's incidents come from disregard of school rules and social parameters.

■ Bernie and Becky Bigfoot meet
ONE out of the FIVE rules for bullying.

Bingo the Dingo / Blingo the Dingo

He or she is not usually a behavior issue, then suddenly they go dingo! Here are the triggers: The student is below grade level in an academic area; they are immature or lack the ability to handle stress; and they do not know how or are unwillingly to ask for help. In other words, Bingo and Blingo would rather be in trouble (and out of the class) than continue to fret over the assignment at hand.

☒ **Bingo does not target victims.** His and Blingo's incidents are random outbursts and the nearest person will do.

☒ **Bingo and Blingo Buck are not an everyday problem.** When the Bingos go "dingo", it will be a shocker. The adults will wonder why it happened and when they discover the reason they might just yell bingo!

☒ **There is no imbalance of power in this scenario.** If another student is involved, it is purely coincidental.

☑☒ **The interaction with others is unwanted,** but lacks an intent to do harm.

☑ **Bingo's transformation is not an accident.** He can no longer stall, and so he huffs, puffs, knocks over desks, or yells at someone nearby. It is an impromptu plan to escape the task he does not want to do by being removed from the classroom. In school suspension is less stressful.

■ Bingo and Blingo meet
1.5 out of the FIVE rules for bullying.

T.A.L.K. - W.A.L.K. -T.E.L.L.

The conflict resolution strategy by school counselor and author David D. Dye Sr. promotes self-esteem, assertiveness, and communication skills. The plan is flexible so it can be used to counteract bullying, bear attacks and other bothersome behaviors. The image below provides each element of the strategy.

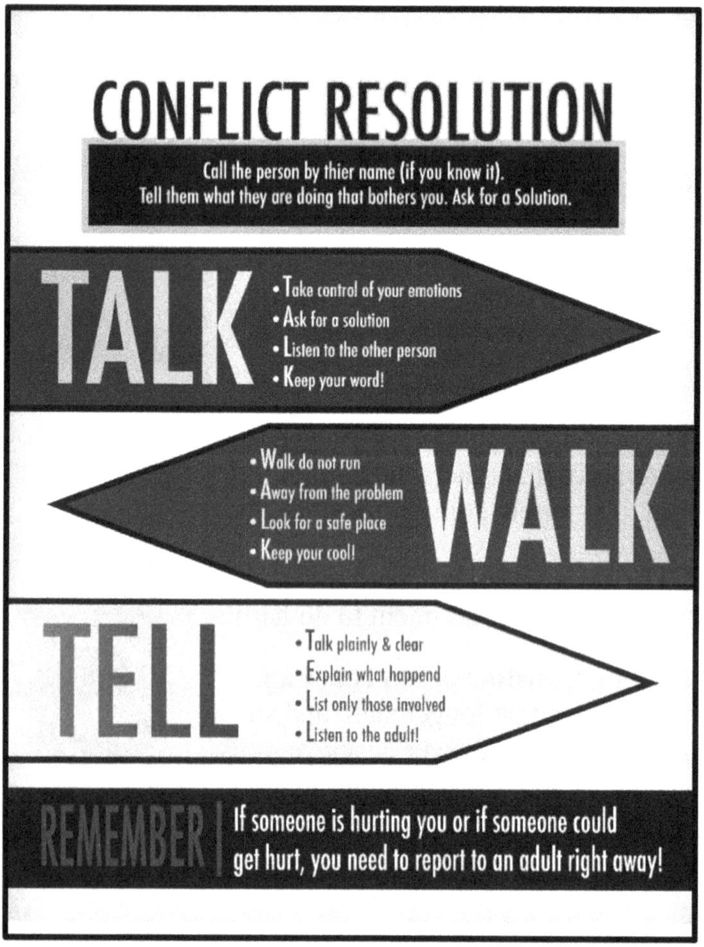

CONFLICT RESOLUTION
Call the person by thier name (if you know it). Tell them what they are doing that bothers you. Ask for a Solution.

TALK
- Take control of your emotions
- Ask for a solution
- Listen to the other person
- Keep your word!

WALK
- Walk do not run
- Away from the problem
- Look for a safe place
- Keep your cool!

TELL
- Talk plainly & clear
- Explain what happened
- List only those involved
- Listen to the adult!

REMEMBER | If someone is hurting you or if someone could get hurt, you need to report to an adult right away!

Like us on Facebook where you can download images to make posters, handouts and lesson materials.

180 Amazing Facts and Crazy Quizzes

Tip for the Student Reader: Read the text beforehand and make sure you can pronounce each word correctly. Ask an adult for help if you come across a word that is difficult.

Notes:
_____
_____
_____
_____
_____
_____
_____

WEEK 1: DAY 1

"Hello, my name is _____ and this is Amazing Facts and Crazy Quizzes."

On TV, bullies always seem the same. They are either big, mean-looking boys or fancy, rich girls with bad attitudes. The amazing fact is that in real life, most students who choose to bully are normal kids[1]. They have friends, like to play, and want to be safe just like you do. Unfortunately, they choose to be mean to those that they think they can control[2]. Each day we will be sharing an amazing fact or crazy quiz about bullying and other bothersome behaviors. Learn the facts and be a buddy, not a bully.

Optional ending: "Until next time, this is _____ with Amazing Facts and Crazy Quizzes."

1. Field, 1996
2. Kaiser, Rasminsky, 2009

WEEK 1: DAY 2

"Hello, my name is _____ and this is Amazing Facts and Crazy Quizzes."

Almost everyone has dealt with bullying[1]. There are two ways to stop bullying. First, we can help the person targeted by bullying to be brave and know how to handle the negative situation. Secondly, we can also help the person who bullies others to stop. We call this strategy, taking the bully by both horns. (Help the person being bothered, and helping the person acting like a bully.)

So, how do you need help? Have you been a victim in the past? Have you been a bully? Are you bully-proof and ready for a happy new school year? Amazing Facts and Crazy Quizzes will help you. Your job is to listen carefully each day and follow the advice.

Optional ending: "Until next time, this is _____ with Amazing Facts and Crazy Quizzes."

WEEK 1: DAY 3 (History of the Word bully)

"Hello, my name is _____ and this is Amazing Facts and Crazy Quizzes."

Do you know what the word *bully* means? Hundreds of years ago the word meant "Sweetheart." Later, it meant a boy's best friend[1]. It is funny how words can change their meaning, just as people can change the way they think and act. The amazing fact is today the word bully is no longer a nice word. What does the word mean to you? Stay tuned to learn more.

Optional ending: "Until next time, this is _____ with Amazing Facts and Crazy Quizzes."

1. Stopbullying.gov | Definition, 2014

WEEK 1: DAY 4

"Hello, my name is _____ and this is Amazing Facts and Crazy Quizzes."

As we learned yesterday, the meaning of the word bully has changed over the years. First, it meant sweetheart, then it meant friend, later the term was used for people who were also called robbers and crooks. In modern times, bully experts developed a definition that explains bullying[2]. It is important that you do not use the word bully until you know the correct definition. Tomorrow we will share this definition with you.

Optional ending: "Until next time, this is _____ with Amazing Facts and Crazy Quizzes."

WEEK 1: DAY 5

"Hello, my name is _____ and this is Amazing Facts and Crazy Quizzes."

Listen up for a simple definition of bullying. Are you listening? **"Bullying is an act of meanness that is on purpose and repeated. The target (also called a victim) feels that they are helpless and cannot defend themselves[3]."** *(Note: repeat the definition)*. Not every mean or bothersome act is bullying. Learn the facts and become a bully expert.

Optional ending: "Until next time, this is _____ with Amazing Facts and Crazy Quizzes."

---

1. Harper, 1999
2. Olweus, 1978
3. Stopbullying.gov | Definition, 2014

Tip for the Student Reader: Stand confident and speak loud and clear. You are sharing important information! Make sure your audience understands you.

Notes:
_____
_____
_____
_____
_____
_____

WEEK 2: DAY 1

"Hello, my name is _____ and this is Amazing Facts and Crazy Quizzes."

Did you know that bullying has rules? The rules come from the definition of bullying and each rule is an amazing fact! Here is Rule #1! **Bullies target their victims[1]**. I repeat: **bullies target their victims[1]**.

Those who bully are not mean to everyone. This is why it is hard to catch them[2]. Report bullying to your teacher, school counselor, or principals. Always tell your parents if someone is picking on you. The Usual Suspects call a boy who bullies, Bully Boy. A Girl who treats others this way is called Buhle Belle.

Optional ending: "Until next time, this is _____ with Amazing Facts and Crazy Quizzes."

---

1. NEA, How to Identify Bullying, 2015
2. Field, 1996

WEEK 2: DAY 2

"Hello, my name is _____ and this is Amazing Facts and Crazy Quizzes."

We know that Rule #1 is: bullies target their victims. Here is Rule #2: **bullying is a constant problem**[1]. Bullying is not something that happens now and then. If someone is acting like Bully Boy or Buhle Belle, he or she will bother you all of the time. Make sure you listen up as we share daily tips on how to handle bullying.

Optional ending: "Until next time, this is _____ with Amazing Facts and Crazy Quizzes."

WEEK 2: DAY 3

"Hello, my name is _____ and this is Amazing Facts and Crazy Quizzes."

We have learned that Rule #1 is: bullies target their victims. Rule #2 is: bullying is a constant problem. Now for Rule #3, Bully Boy and Buhle Belle think he or she has power over the person they pick on[2]. This is also called an imbalance of power. I repeat, Bully Boy and Buhle Belle think they have **power over their target.**

Optional ending: "Until next time, this is _____ with Amazing Facts and Crazy Quizzes."

---

1. Dake, Price, Telljohaun, 2003
2. Olweus, Mortimore, 1993,

WEEK 2: DAY 4

"Hello, my name is _____ and this is Amazing Facts and Crazy Quizzes."

Here is bully rule #4: **bullying is an unwanted aggression[1] and meant to do harm.** Bully Boy and Buhle Belle want to be mean and intend to do harm[2] with their words and actions. Just in case you do not know, the term "aggression" is defined, "To be rude, hurtful or mean."

When playing a sport or a game at recess things can get rough. The player wants this type of action or should expect it to get rough if they choose to play football, basketball or a game like "tag." These rough actions are not bullying. Bullying is an unwanted aggression and meant to do harm.

Optional ending: "Until next time, this is _____ with Amazing Facts and Crazy Quizzes."

WEEK 2: DAY 5

"Hello, my name is _____ and this is Amazing Facts and Crazy Quizzes."

Not every problem is bullying. So remember the five rules. Bullies target the person they pick on. It is a constant problem. It involves an imbalance of power. Bullying is an unwanted aggression meant to do harm. The fifth rule is: **bullying is not an accident; it is on purpose[1].** Remember, bullying is totally uncool.

Optional ending: "Until next time, this is _____ with Amazing Facts and Crazy Quizzes."

---

1. Stopbullying.gov | Definition, 2014
2. NEA, How to Identify Bullying, 2015
3. Fagan, Mazerolle, 2011

Tip for the Student Reader: A web address is read differently than a sentence. The web address: www.stopbulling.gov/kid is read w.w.w. Stop-bullying (dot) gov (forward slash) kid.

Notes:

_____
_____
_____
_____
_____
_____
_____

WEEK 3: DAY 1

"Hello, my name is _____ and this is Amazing Facts and Crazy Quizzes."

The website www.stopbullying.gov is an accurate and useful place to find bully information. For videos, games and more, look up www.stopbulling.gov/kid. Knowledge is power. You do not have to wait for an adult to tell you. Become a bully expert.

Optional ending: "Until next time, this is _____ with Amazing Facts and Crazy Quizzes."

WEEK 3: DAY 2

"Hello, my name is _____ and this is Amazing Facts and Crazy Quizzes."

It is impossible to spot a bully by looking at them[1]. Acting like Bully Boy and Buhle Belle is an action and not a look on someone's face. You cannot know if a boy is a bully just because he is tall or strong looking. Likewise, just because a girl is popular does not mean she will pick on shy girls. Bullies can only be "seen" while being mean to someone. This is why victims must make a report to an adult in school[2]. Always tell your parents when you have this problem. If you do not TELL, the bully may never stop.

Optional ending: "Until next time, this is _____ with Amazing Facts and Crazy Quizzes."

WEEK 3: DAY 3

"Hello, my name is _____ and this is Amazing Facts and Crazy Quizzes."

According to experts, there are two types of bullies. First, there is the serial bully who wants to hurt others. The other kind of bully is the ordinary person. The studies say the "ordinary person" does 96% of bullying[1]. It makes sense then; it is up to ordinary people to stop bullying too. If it's not cool, don't do it in school!

Optional ending: "Until next time, this is _____ with Amazing Facts and Crazy Quizzes."

---

1. Hoover, Stenhjam, 2003
2. Field. 1996

WEEK 3: DAY 4 (History of the Word Bully)

"Hello, my name is ___ and this is Amazing Facts and Crazy Quizzes."

In a book published in 1915, the author described the crew of a sailing ship as tough bullies when things were good. When the way turned rough, they turned out to be cowards[1]. Bullies may look tough, but they want an easy target[2]. Do not give them what they want. The strategy, TALK-WALK-TELL can help.

The first part, TALK, will show bullies that you are not an easy push over. Look the person in the eyes, stand tall, and use a calm, but firm voice. Call the person by name (if you know it), tell him or her what they are doing that bothers you, and ask them to stop. Since you already know they are trying to be mean, slowly turn and walk away after you have spoken to them.

Optional ending: "Until next time, this is _____ with Amazing Facts and Crazy Quizzes."

WEEK 3: DAY 5 (Girls Bully Differently)

"Hello, my name is _____ and this is Amazing Facts and Crazy Quizzes."

One way Buhle Belle likes to be mean is to make the person she is picking on feel left out of the group. She might tell him or her they are not welcome. She might say that "others" do not want to play with them[3]. Be a hero and not a zero, if you see someone bullied liked this, crash the party. Ask the victim to play with you somewhere else and walk away together.

Optional ending: "Until next time, this is _____ with Amazing Facts and Crazy Quizzes."

1. Kephart, 1915   2. Anderson, Swiatowy, 2008
3. National Crime Prevention Council, 2015

Tip for the Student Reader: The superscript numbers that look like this[1] refer to the references at the bottom of the page. These numbers[1] should not be read.

Notes:
_____
_____
_____
_____
_____
_____
_____

WEEK 4: DAY 1

"Hello, my name is _____ and this is Amazing Facts and Crazy Quizzes."

    Some people think that bullying only happens if there is punching, shoving, or kicking. This is not correct. The most common form of bullying is name-calling or using hurtful words[1]. Making fun of someone is rude and mean. If you do not have something good to say, say nothing at all. Remember to be kind with your words.

Optional ending: "Until next time, this is _____ with Amazing Facts and Crazy Quizzes."

---

1. Cohn, Canter, 1999

WEEK 4: DAY 2 (Crazy Quiz #1)

"Hello, my name is _____ and this is Amazing Facts and Crazy Quizzes."

Listen to this story and decide if it is the proper way to use TALK.

Ping is in the restroom and Ben calls him a name and says his shoes smell. Ben is always saying mean things to Ping. Today Ping decides he must stand up for himself. He looks Ben in the eyes and stands with his hands to his side. He calmly says, "Ben you like being mean to me. I would like you to stop. Besides, my shoes smell like pizza, and I love pizza."

Is this a good example of using TALK? The answer is yes. Ping called the person by name, explained what he was doing that was bothersome and then asked him to stop. Ping also used humor. Humor is a good way to relieve tension.

Optional ending: "Until next time, this is _____ with Amazing Facts and Crazy Quizzes."

WEEK 4: DAY 3 (Conflict Resolution: TALK-WALK-TELL)

"Hello, my name is _____ and this is Amazing Facts and Crazy Quizzes."

TALK, WALK, and TELL is a strategy to help resolve problems. If someone is bothering you, calmly TALK to him or her and use this strategy: T stands for **T**ake control of your emotions, A stands for **A**sk them calmly to stop, L stands for **L**isten to what they say (you might be bothering them too) K is **K**eep your promises[1].

Optional ending: "Until next time, this is _____ with Amazing Facts and Crazy Quizzes."

1. Lereya, Samara, Wolke, 2013

WEEK 4: DAY 4

"Hello, my name is _____ and this is Amazing Facts and Crazy Quizzes."

Bullies want to control their target. In many cases, they want to make their victim react with strong emotions[2]. Do not give the bully what they want. Do not show that you are sad, frustrated, or angry. Calmly use TALK and then confidentially walk away[3].

Optional ending: "Until next time, this is _____ with Amazing Facts and Crazy Quizzes."

WEEK 4: DAY 5 (Conflict Resolution: TALK-WALK-TELL)

"Hello, my name is _____ and this is Amazing Facts and Crazy Quizzes."

School Counselor David D. Dye created TALK-WALK-TELL as a skill to use when someone is bothering you. The first step is to talk to the person bothering you. Call them by name if you know it. Tell them calmly what they are doing that bothers you. Ask for a solution. Remember, if someone is hurting you or someone else, skip TALK and go as quickly as you can to an adult and report it.

Optional ending: "Until next time, this is _____ with Amazing Facts and Crazy Quizzes."

---

1. Fagan, Mazerolle, 2011
2. Beane, 2014

Tip for the Student Reader: If you want to be the very best spokesperson, ask someone you trust to listen to you read and ask them if they understand you.

Notes:
_____
_____
_____
_____
_____
_____
_____

WEEK 5: DAY 1 (History of the word Bully)

"Hello, my name is _____ and this is Amazing Facts and Crazy Quizzes."

Another definition for the word bully from a few hundred years ago meant a loud-mouthed person or swashbuckler[1]. During this time, people called pirates and thieves bully-ruffians[2]. Pirates attacked weaker vessels. They sailed away from well-armed ships. Even then, bullies looked for an easy target and were cowards in their heart.

Optional ending: "Until next time, this is _____ with Amazing Facts and Crazy Quizzes."

1. Peters, 2010
2. Beane, 2014

WEEK 5: DAY 2 (Conflict Resolution: TALK-WALK-TELL)

"Hello, my name is _____ and this is Amazing Facts and Crazy Quizzes."

What do you do if you use TALK and the person troubling you reacts in a mean way? WALK away immediately. The conversation is over. <u>W</u>alk do not run- <u>A</u>way from the person- <u>L</u>ook for a safe place near friends or an adult- <u>K</u>eep your cool. If a person is talking mean or arguing, you do not have to listen to them. Staying only gives them more power. WALK confidently away[2].

Optional ending: "Until next time, this is _____ with Amazing Facts and Crazy Quizzes."

WEEK 5: DAY 3

"Hello, my name is _____ and this is Amazing Facts and Crazy Quizzes."

Learning about bullying is very important. Listen carefully to the facts. Learn to tell the difference between bullying and other bad deeds. Do not use the word bully unless it fits the rules.

Optional ending: "Until next time, this is _____ with Amazing Facts and Crazy Quizzes."

WEEK 5: DAY 4 (The Herd and the Hero)

"Hello, my name is ___ and this is Amazing Facts and Crazy Quizzes."

Bullying often happens when adults are not close enough to hear. Those who bully do like other students to watch[1]. If you are a bystander in the crowd, you have a choice to make. You can be part of the herd and help the one bullying or you can just watch in silence. Either way you are part of the problem and not the solution. A third choice is to help the person being bullied. If friends decide to stand together, the bully will be outnumbered and will feel the pressure to stop. Make your presence count: Be a hero, not a zero!

Optional ending: "Until next time, this is _____ with Amazing Facts and Crazy Quizzes."

WEEK 5: DAY 5

"Hello, my name is ___ and this is Amazing Facts and Crazy Quizzes."

Here are suggestions from Dr. Beane, an expert on bullying[2].

- Look confident by standing tall and holding your head up.
- Do not cry or run off. Don't look sad and don't look angry.
- Move closer to the person, *turn sideways, with your right foot pointing forward.
- Hold your arms beside your body. Don't hold your arms up like you want to fight.
- Make eye contact.
- Make your assertive comment and then walk away confidently.

Optional ending: "Until next time, this is _____ with Amazing Facts and Crazy Quizzes."

*This position is a common defensive stance. Look up CPI techniques on the internet.

1. Dake, Price, Telljohaun, 2003
2. Beane, 2014

Tip for the Student Reader: Respect the punctuation. Periods (.) are like a stop sign. Take a short break at each period. You might take a breath at the period. Keeping the sentences separated by a short break helps keep the meaning clear.

Notes:
_____
_____
_____
_____
_____
_____
_____

WEEK 6: DAY 1 (Crazy Quiz 2)

"Hello, my name is _____ and this is Amazing Facts and Crazy Quizzes."

Listen to this story and decide if it is the right way to use WALK.

Ralph decides he is going to use TWT on the boy who keeps picking on him. He stands facing his foe, turns sideways and looks in the bully's eyes as he says, "I don't like it when you call me names." The boy bullying him replies with a loud grumpy voice, "I don't care." Ralph quickly turns and runs away.

Is this the right way to use WALK: Yes, or No? The answer is No. Running away will make the bully want to chase you and it shows that the bully has succeeded in controlling your emotions and actions. Remember WALK stands for **W**alk do not run- **A**way from the problem- **L**ook for a safe place- **K**eep your cool.

Optional ending: "Until next time, this is _____ with Amazing Facts and Crazy Quizzes."

WEEK 6: DAY 2

"Hello, my name is _____ and this is Amazing Facts and Crazy Quizzes."

According to experts, individuals who bully are more likely to go to jail when they grow up[1]. Think about what you are doing when you act like Bully Boy or Buhle Belle. Also, think about what you will become. Your future starts now!

Optional ending: "Until next time, this is _____ with Amazing Facts and Crazy Quizzes."

WEEK 6: DAY 3 (History of the Word Bully)

"Hello, my name is _____ and this is Amazing Facts and Crazy Quizzes."

President Teddy Roosevelt, the 26th President of the United States, used the term "bully" to mean "first-rate." He would often say, "Bully for you" when giving a compliment[2]. The word bully has gone from meaning something positive to meaning something very negative. Now days a bully wants to feel first-rate by controlling others.

Optional ending: "Until next time, this is _____ with Amazing Facts and Crazy Quizzes."

---

1. Seely, Tombari, Bennett and Dunkle, 2011.
2. Peters, 2010

WEEK 6: DAY 4 (Conflict Resolution: TALK-WALK-TELL)

"Hello, my name is _____ and this is Amazing Facts and Crazy Quizzes."

TALK will solve many clashes before they become a problem. It helps us know exactly what is going on. WALK will end the conflict before it starts. Sometimes, the best made plans do not work. A bully might keep picking on you. If they do, TELL an adult, and remember what TELL stands for: T is for **T**alk clearly and plainly, E is for **E**xplain what happened. L stands for **L**ist the people involved. The next L stands for **L**isten to the adult's advice. Always talk to your parents about problems like this.

Optional ending: "Until next time, this is _____ with Amazing Facts and Crazy Quizzes."

WEEK 6: DAY 5 (Rule #2 Review: A Constant Problem.)

"Hello, my name is _____ and this is Amazing Facts and Crazy Quizzes."

Bullying is not a one-time event. If a person sees you every day and only bothers you sometimes, something else is going on. This does not fit the rules of bullying. You can find out what kind of behavior it is with the free app by Mr. Dye. The Usual Suspect ID Cards is an app is for iPad, Android phones, and tablets.

Optional ending: "Until next time, this is _____ with Amazing Facts and Crazy Quizzes."

Tip for the Student Reader: Do not say the word (Pause) in a parenthesis. It is a direction for you to give a short break to let the audience think before you reveal the answer.

Notes:
_____
_____
_____
_____
_____
_____
_____

WEEK 7: DAY 1 (Crazy Quiz # 2)

"Hello, my name is _____ and this is Amazing Facts and Crazy Quizzes."

Is Bernie a bully? There is a boy in your class. He is a little taller than everyone else is. He is full of energy. He is a likable person, but every day he plows over different people in the hallway. He bumps into classmates when he is lining up. Sometimes he even kicks your feet under the desk. Is Bernie acting like Bully Boy? Think about the five rules of bullying. (Pause) The answer is; no. Bernie is not a bully. He is what The Usual Suspects call a Bigfoot. Because he is clumsy and does not always pay attention, he sometimes looks like a bully.

Bernie and Bertha Bigfoot are part of the Usual Suspects. He or she may be uncoordinated because of growth spurts. They may also have a problem with paying attention and being alert. Use TALK-WALK-TELL if you are having a Bigfoot.

Optional ending: "Until next time, this is _____ with Amazing Facts and Crazy Quizzes."

WEEK 7: DAY 2 (Conflict Resolution: TALK-WALK-TELL)

"Hello, my name is _____ and this is Amazing Facts and Crazy Quizzes."

In the plan TALK, the "L" stands for Listen to the other person. This is very important. What should you do if the person bothering you wants to talk calmly about the problem? If you listen to the other person, you might find out how to solve the issue. You might even find out that YOU are part of the problem and need to change a few things. We should never assume that it is always the other person's fault. Sometimes we might be the cause of the conflict.

Optional ending: "Until next time, this is _____ with Amazing Facts and Crazy Quizzes."

WEEK 7: DAY 3 (Rule #1 Review: Bullies Target their Victims.)

"Hello, my name is _____ and this is Amazing Facts and Crazy Quizzes."

If bullies target their victims, how do they treat those they do not target? Here is an amazing fact: students who bully are not mean to everyone. That's right! Bully Boy and Buhle Belle are not mean to everyone. They could be nice to other people. They could have friends or even be popular. This is why bullies are hard to catch. It is everyone's responsibility to make a stand against bullying[1].

Optional ending: "Until next time, this is _____ with Amazing Facts and Crazy Quizzes."

---

1. Juvonen, Wang, Espinoza, 2013

WEEK 7: DAY 4 (Conflict Resolution: TALK-WALK-TELL)

"Hello, my name is _____ and this is Amazing Facts and Crazy Quizzes."

If a person is hurting you, or someone else, do not use TWT. Go to an adult as fast as you can. If a bully wants to fight, walk away from him or her. If someone grabs you, yell "stop" or "no" and yank away at the same time. Yelling may shock the attacker just enough to escape[2]. Ask your teachers and parents what you should do in this situation. Be prepared ahead of time.

Optional ending: "Until next time, this is _____ with Amazing Facts and Crazy Quizzes."

WEEK 7: DAY 5 (Crazy Quiz #3)

"Hello, my name is _____ and this is Amazing Facts and Crazy Quizzes."

Billy is always bothering you. He pokes you and follows you around, smiling every step of the way. At recess, he tries to play what you are playing. At lunch, he sits at the same table as you and wants to share food and snacks. If you do not pay attention to him, he might tug on your shirt or even pull your hair. (Pause)

Is Billy a bully? Remember the five rules of bullying. The answer is no. There is not an imbalance of power and there is no intent to do harm. Billy is, however, part of the Usual Suspects. His name is Billy Badger. He wants to be your friend, but does not know how. Use **TALK-WALK-TELL** if Billy is bothering you.

Optional ending: "Until next time, this is _____ with Amazing Facts and Crazy Quizzes."

1. Juvonen, Wang, Espinoza, 2013
2. Steiger, 1987

Tip for the Student Reader: Changing the pitch or tone of your voice makes it easier to listen to your reading. This is called inflection in your voice. Ask a sponsor or perhaps your music teacher to help you with this.

Notes:
_____
_____
_____
_____
_____
_____
_____

WEEK 8: DAY 1 (Target or Victim?)

"Hello, my name is _____ and this is Amazing Facts and Crazy Quizzes."

It is very important how an individual responds the first time a person tries to bully them. This determines what the bully does next. If the target becomes upset, the bully will mark them as an easy target. They will continue to pick on them. If the target does not become upset, the bully will most likely leave them alone[1]. Use a strategy like TALK-WALK-TELL. Let the bully know you are not an easy target.

Optional ending: "Until next time, this is _____ with Amazing Facts and Crazy Quizzes."

1. Lereya, Samara, Wolke, 2013

WEEK 8: DAY 2 (Revenge and Getting Even)

"Hello, my name is _____ and this is Amazing Facts and Crazy Quizzes."

Boomerang bullying is when the target finds a way to have power over the bully. The victim starts revenge on the bully. Listen to this case story: Mandy is smart in math, but Adam is not. Mandy is mean to him every day and makes fun of his poor grades. Adam knows it is true and suffers in silence. He is too embarrassed to let the teacher know a girl is picking on him. At recess, he realizes that he is bigger and he has the power in his hands. He starts his revenge and picks on her. Being smart, Mandy reports him. He receives consequences for being a bully while Mandy is the real problem and gets away with it. It is not your fault the other person is being mean. Do not be too embarrassed to use TALK, WALK and TELL.

Optional ending: "Until next time, this is _____ with Amazing Facts and Crazy Quizzes."

WEEK 8: DAY 3 (The Usual Suspects ID Cards)

"Hello, my name is _____ and this is Amazing Facts and Crazy Quizzes."

The Usual Suspects ID Cards is a free App for iPad, Android phones and tablets. It teaches about bullying and other bothersome behaviors. Learn about Bigfoot, Badger and more. It is a free download, but ask your parents before downloading it. It's your job to become bully-proof! Start today.

Optional ending: "Until next time, this is _____ with Amazing Facts and Crazy Quizzes."

WEEK 8: DAY 4

"Hello, my name is _____ and this is Amazing Facts and Crazy Quizzes."

If it is not bullying, then what do you call it? Remember the rules of bullying: "Bullying is on purpose. It is repeated over and over again. It is unwanted aggression. It is meant to do harm. There is an imbalance of power." Now, you know the rules. What do you call it if the action does not fit the rules? Is the person bothering you still a bully? The amazing fact is no. If the behavior does not fit the rules of bullying, it must be something else! Stay tuned to learn more about Bigfoots, Badgers, and Bears. Remember, not every bothersome behavior is bullying. Find out more to bully proof yourself and your friends.

Optional ending: "Until next time, this is _____ with Amazing Facts and Crazy Quizzes."

WEEK 8: DAY 5

"Hello, my name is _____ and this is Amazing Facts and Crazy Quizzes."

Knowledge is power. Students who are victims of bullying tend to play that role repeatedly throughout their lives[1]. Stop the cycle now. Ask your teacher or school counselor how you can become bully-proof.

Optional ending: "Until next time, this is _____ with Amazing Facts and Crazy Quizzes."

---

1. Elliott, 1993

Tip for the Student Reader: When you come to the word (repeat) in parenthesis, do not read the word (repeat) out loud. This is instructions to you to re-read a sentence or thought. In addition, when you see __ call it a blank. He ___ (blanked) the test.

Notes:
_____
_____
_____
_____
_____

WEEK 9: DAY 1 (Crazy Quiz # 4)

"Hello, my name is _____ and this is Amazing Facts and Crazy Quizzes."

Do you know the five rules of bullying? Here is a crazy quiz to check your knowledge. It is okay to work in groups or with your desk buddies. I'll wait a few seconds as you get your team together (pause ten seconds) Okay, here is the quiz?

1. Is this a rule of bullying? Bullies **target** their victims. Yes, or No (Pause) the answer is yes, Rule # 1 states: Bullies are not mean to everyone. They target the person the pick on.

2. Is this a rule of bullying? Bullying is a **little** problem. Yes, or No (Pause) the answer is no, Rule # 2 states: Bullying is a <u>constant</u> problem.

3. What does "<u>imbalance of power</u>" mean? Rule #3 states: Bullying involves an <u>imbalance of power</u> in favor of the bully. (Pause) Imbalance of power means that the victim feels helpless and thinks he or she cannot defend themselves.

Optional ending: "Until next time, this is _____ with Amazing Facts and Crazy Quizzes."

WEEK 9: DAY 2

"Hello, my name is _____ and this is Amazing Facts and Crazy Quizzes."

Teachers and staff are required to take bullying seriously. You may report to any teacher or adult worker. An investigation will follow. Be ready to use TELL as a guideline. "T" stands for **Talk clearly and slowly.** "E" stands for **Explain what happened.** Give details that are important to the bullying. Do not include details about other things. "L" is for **List only those involved.** Again, do not talk about others who did not bully you. Stay on topic when you report the problem. The last "L" stands for **Listen to the adult's advice**. They may help you to avoid trouble in the future.

Optional ending: "Until next time, this is _____ with Amazing Facts and Crazy Quizzes."

WEEK 9: DAY 3 (Rule #3 Review)

"Hello, my name is _____ and this is Amazing Facts and Crazy Quizzes."

Bullying always involves an imbalance of power. This means the victim thinks he or she cannot defend himself or herself. This kind of thinking needs to change. It takes courage to report a problem like bullying. The person bullying may tell you they will hurt you if you tell. Think about this, they are already hurting you. Telling may be the only way to stop them. Some students do not trust their teacher to help. Also, report the problem to the school principal and your parents.

Optional ending: "Until next time, this is _____ with Amazing Facts and Crazy Quizzes."

WEEK 9: DAY 4 (Rule # 4 Review)

"Hello, my name is _____ and this is Amazing Facts and Crazy Quizzes."

Bullying is unwanted aggression. Aggression is when someone hits, kicks or pushes. There are both boys and girls who like to play rough. The Usual Suspects call this kind of behavior being a Buck or Buckette. You have seen pictures of two young deer (also called bucks) locking horns and fighting. The deer fight to exercise and show their strength. There are people who like to wrestle and fight for fun and exercise too. In their own mind, they are not being mean; they are trying to have fun. Tell Buck or Buckette that you do not like to play rough. Give them other suggestions on how to play. Use TWT. Tell an adult immediately, if needed.

Optional ending: "Until next time, this is _____ with Amazing Facts and Crazy Quizzes."

WEEK 9: DAY 5 (Meet the Usual Suspect called the Bear)

"Hello, my name is _____ and this is Amazing Facts and Crazy Quizzes."

While it is impossible to tell who a bully is by looking at them, it is easy to spot the character that the Usual Suspects call the Bear. Buster and Baddie Bear tend to frown, scowl, and let everyone know they are in a grizzly mood. Bullies target individual, while the Bear is pretty much mean and grumpy to everyone. Bullies want to control your emotions, but Buster or Baddie Bear want to hurt you physically if you cross their path at the wrong time. When a Bear attacks, do not try to use TALK, instead WALK away from the Bear, and report them immediately.

Tip for the Student Reader: As you read a Crazy Quiz, make sure to say the letters for each choice. A) = /A/. B) = /B/. This will help the listener stay on track.

Notes:
_____
_____
_____
_____
_____
_____
_____

WEEK 10: DAY 1 (Crazy Quiz #5)

"Hello, my name is _____ and this is Amazing Facts and Crazy Quizzes."

Bullying involves an imbalance of power. Which of the following is an imbalance of power used in bullying? A) Ken reads two grade levels higher than Jess. B) Beth is a great athlete and her PE partner, Kate is clumsy. C) Penelope is very popular and her locker buddy has few friends. (Pause) Which of these did you choose? The answer is all of the above. An imbalance of power could be size, talent, or academics. Remember, bullying is a choice. Use your power to be a buddy.

Optional ending: "Until next time, this is _____ with Amazing Facts and Crazy Quizzes."

WEEK 10: DAY 2

"Hello, my name is _____ and this is Amazing Facts and Crazy Quizzes."

Sometimes bullying is in the mind of the beholder. That means that some students think others are bullying them when they are not. For example, Jimmy thinks Peter is out to bully him. The way Jimmy sees it, Peter almost ran him over in the hall and now he keeps staring at him in class. Jimmy feels stressed and afraid.

What really happened? Jimmy does not realize that sometimes he makes mistakes and is at fault. Back in the hallway, Jimmy was daydreaming and not paying attention. He stepped in front of Peter, who then bumped into him. (Peter was the victim not Jimmy). Now in class, Peter is watching the clock because he is excited about pizza for lunch. The clock is on the wall right behind Jimmy's desk. Jimmy is thinking like a victim and is wrong about Peter.

Optional ending: "Until next time, this is __ with Amazing Facts and Crazy Quizzes."

WEEK 10: DAY 3 (Rule #1 Review)

"Hello, my name is _____ and this is Amazing Facts and Crazy Quizzes."

If Bullies target their victims, why do they pick on that certain person? There are several possible reasons why those who bully choose their victim. One possible reason is the target may remind the bully of his or her own weaknesses[1]. Without knowing it, bullies sometime try to "get even" with their own self. You can stop bullying from the inside out: rise above the urge to bully. Ask your school counselor for help.

Optional ending: "Until next time, this is __ with Amazing Facts and Crazy Quizzes."

1. McLeod, 2008

WEEK 10: DAY 4

"Hello, my name is _____ and this is Amazing Facts and Crazy Quizzes."

A bully may be able to take your lunch money, but he or she cannot take away your self-esteem. First Lady, Eleanor Roosevelt said. "No one can make you feel inferior without your consent[1]." How you react to a bully is up to you. Determine in your heart to be a Victor and not a Victim. Sometimes the person bullying is bigger. Sometimes they have a herd with them. Sometimes there is nothing you can do to stop them. This does not make you weak. Show your strength and your smarts by reporting the problem. Tell a trusted adult. Do not face the problem alone and help us stop bullying in our school.

Optional ending: "Until next time, this is __ with Amazing Facts and Crazy Quizzes."

WEEK 10: DAY 5 (The Hero and the Herd)

"Hello, my name is _____ and this is Amazing Facts and Crazy Quizzes."

It is always best to have a plan. Talk with your friends. Agree ahead of time about what you will do if you see bullying. Plan ahead of time to stand with the victim and agree to tell the bully to stop[2]. Remember to act like a hero when you talk to the aggressor. Remain calm, but be firm and do not use inappropriate words. Use TALK as a guideline: 1) call the person by name (if you know it), 2) tell them what they are doing that is bothersome, and 3) ask them to stop. In this situation, it is important to let the bully know that you will be reporting their actions to an adult.

Optional ending: "Until next time, this is _____ with Amazing Facts and Crazy Quizzes."

1. Goodreads, 2015
2. Stopbullying.gov | Bystander, 2014

Tip for the Student Reader: Please do not read the references at the bottom of the page out loud.

Notes:
_____
_____
_____
_____
_____
_____

WEEK 11: DAY 1 (Rule #1 Review)

"Hello, my name is _____ and this is Amazing Facts and Crazy Quizzes."

If Bullies target their victims, why do they pick that certain person? Sometimes those who bully choose a target because he or she sees a trait they think is strange or different. This is the meanest way to bully. A person cannot change how tall they are, or how big their nose or feet may be. Bully Boy might make fun of a person wearing glasses. Buhle Belle might pick on a person with freckles or braces. The problem is not with how the target looks. The problem is with how the bully thinks and acts. One amazing fact is bullies often have things about themselves that can be made fun of too[1].

Remember, we cannot change most things about ourselves, but there are some things we can change to be healthier. If fixing your hair or using deodorant will make you less of a target, do it. It will also make your friends happier too.

Optional ending: "Until next time, this is _____ with Amazing Facts and Crazy Quizzes."

WEEK 11: DAY 2 (Rule #1 Review)

"Hello, my name is _____ and this is Amazing Facts and Crazy Quizzes."

If Bullies target their victims, why do they pick on that certain person? One reason could be that the targeted person reminds the bully of the individual who used to pick on them. Their bad memories pick out the victim. They seek revenge on the other person that bullied them[1]. (A person they are afraid to face.) Think of how you treat others. Make sure you are not letting past problems control your emotions. Ask yourself, why am I acting this way? Then ask a friend or adult to help you stop.

Optional ending: "Until next time, this is _____ with Amazing Facts and Crazy Quizzes."

WEEK 11: DAY 3 (Crazy Quiz #6)

"Hello, my name is _____ and this is Amazing Facts and Crazy Quizzes."

Bingo is a cool kid and everyone seems to like him. One day in math class, he starts yelling at Betsy who was sitting beside him and then dumps over his desk. Paper went flying everywhere. Is Bingo being a bully to Betsy, or is something different happening? (Pause) The answer is no. Bingo is not a bully, he does not fit any of the rules, but he is one of The Usual Suspects, Bingo the Dingo. He or she would rather be in trouble than struggling with math.

Optional ending: "Until next time, this is _____ with Amazing Facts and Crazy Quizzes."

---

1. McLeod, 2008

WEEK 11: DAY 4 (Bullying is in the Eyes of the Beholder)

"Hello, my name is _____ and this is Amazing Facts and Crazy Quizzes."

You think Sandy is a bully, but maybe you need to rethink what is going on. The facts tell the truth. Sandy accidentally knocked over your milk. Instead of accepting her apology, you keep making up things in your head about her. You imagine that she is being mean to you. The truth is, she has done nothing to you on purpose, yet, you have been very rude to her. Maybe, you are the bully and need to say you are sorry. Use TALK to solve problems like this. **T** stands for Take control of your emotions- **A** stands for Ask them calmly to stop- **L** stands for Listen to what they say (you might be bothering them too)- **K** is Keep your promises.

Optional ending: "Until next time, this is _____ with Amazing Facts and Crazy Quizzes."

WEEK 11: DAY 5 (Rule #1 Review)

"Hello, my name is _____ and this is Amazing Facts and Crazy Quizzes."

Sometimes Bully Boy picks on an individual because the target reminds them of something they fear could happen to them. For example, a straight "A" student fears failing. A student who is making poor grades becomes their target. Another example is a person who is afraid of gaining weight might target a person who is overweight. The mind of the bully is complicated. The amazing fact is simple; it is not your fault if a bully picks on you. The problem is with the person being mean. Sometimes asking the person why they are being mean solves the issue. It also helps us realize that those who bully are people too.

Optional ending: "Until next time, this is _____ with Amazing Facts and Crazy Quizzes."

Tip for the Student Reader: Stand confident and speak loud and clear. You are sharing important information! Make sure your audience understands you.

Notes:
_____
_____
_____
_____
_____
_____
_____

WEEK 12: DAY 1

"Hello, my name is _____ and this is Amazing Facts and Crazy Quizzes."

Cyber Bullying is when bullying happens online. Nowadays, "online" can also mean on your smartphone. It is easy to stop cyber bullying on your phone. Do not give your phone numbers to mean people. Do not link your phone to sites like Facebook, Twitter or Instagram. Block the number of the person that is bothering you. Before you can do this, however, you must tell your parents and show them the messages. If it is a student at school, show your teacher the messages too. A screen shot can be taken on some phones. Make the text screen a picture that your parents can save on their phone.

Optional ending: "Until next time, this is _____ with Amazing Facts and Crazy Quizzes."

WEEK 12: DAY 2 (Crazy Quiz #7)

"Hello, my name is _____ and this is Amazing Facts and Crazy Quizzes."

Something happened on the playground and Marcie needs to report it. Choose the best way to follow TELL.

A) Marcie talks about several students who were not part of the problem.
B) Marcie is so excited she is yelling the same thing repeatedly.
C) Marcie talks clearly and explains exactly what happen.

Which one did you choose? The answer is (Pause) C (Read C again).

Optional ending "Until next time, this is __ with Amazing Facts and Crazy Quizzes."

WEEK 12: DAY 3 (The Hero and the Herd)

"Hello, my name is _____ and this is Amazing Facts and Crazy Quizzes."
What do you call a group of people who gather when there is trouble? The Usual Suspect calls it a herd. Remember, bullies and victims hang out in the herd; however, heroes stand out in a crowd. If you decide to be a hero, be a friend to the victim if you can. They need someone to show them that they have worth as a human being. Your friendship could change their life forever[1].

If you see a person being bullied, walk up to the target and call them by name if you know it. Ask them to leave with you. Both of you should walk away with confidence. Encourage the victim to tell an adult about the bully problem.

Optional ending: "Until next time, this is _____ with Amazing Facts and Crazy Quizzes."

1. U.S. Department of Health & Human Services, 2014

WEEK 12: DAY 4 (Rule #3 Review)

"Hello, my name is _____ and this is Amazing Facts and Crazy Quizzes."

Bullying involves an imbalance of power. Most people think of size. Smaller children pick on bigger kids every day. Teachers and students need to be aware of this. The power could be size, grades, popularity, and more. The power does not have to be real. Most of the time, the person bullying only thinks they have power. The target can show strength by using TALK, WALK and TELL. They can also show power by not becoming visibly upset.

WEEK 12: DAY 5 (Girls Bully Differently)

"Hello, my name is _____ and this is Amazing Facts and Crazy Quizzes."

Buhle Belle loves to spread rumors about her target[2]. These rumors are hateful and untrue. If you hear a rumor going around stop if you can. Ask the person to stop saying mean things. Report it to your teacher or another adult at school you trust.

Optional ending: "Until next time, this is _____ with Amazing Facts and Crazy Quizzes."

---

1. National Crime Prevention Council, 2015

Tip for the Student Reader: A web address is read differently than a sentence. The web address: www.stopbulling.gov/kid is read w.w.w. stop-bullying (dot) gov (forward slash) kid.

Notes:
_____
_____
_____
_____
_____
_____
_____

WEEK 13: DAY 1

"Hello, my name is _____ and this is Amazing Facts and Crazy Quizzes."

What do you call a person who laughs while the bully is picking on a target? Researchers call them bully-assistants[1]. Some call them "passive bullies"[2]. They do not usually start a bullying incident. They are willing and happy to join in when someone else does. If you are laughing *with* the bully that means you are laughing *at* the victim. That makes you just another bully in the herd[3]. Be a leader and not a follower. Think about your actions.

Optional ending: "Until next time, this is _____ with Amazing Facts and Crazy Quizzes."

---

1. Stopbullying.gov | The Roles Kids Play, 2014
2. Kansas State Department of Education, 2014,
3. Stopbullying.gov/kids | What You Can Do, 2014

WEEK 13: DAY 2

"Hello, my name is _____ and this is Amazing Facts and Crazy Quizzes."

The website www.stopbullying.gov gives this advice if someone is bothering you: "Look at the kid bullying you and tell him or her to stop in a calm, clear voice. You can also try to laugh it off. This works best if joking is easy for you. It could catch the kid bullying you off guard[3]." Character Academy calls this strategy, TALK-WALK-TELL. It is very important to TALK to the person bothering you. This lets them know that you are not an easy push over. Calmly TALK and then confidently WALK away. If they continue, TELL an adult at school and report it to your parents.

Optional ending: "Until next time, this is _____ with Amazing Facts and Crazy Quizzes."

WEEK 13: DAY 3

"Hello, my name is _____ and this is Amazing Facts and Crazy Quizzes."

A study showed that an audience was present 88% of the time bullying took place. That meant that 88 times out of a 100 there were other students watching the bully being mean[1]. When you see bullying taking place, do not be part of the herd. If you see bullying, most of the time that bully has no power over you. Show kindness to the person being bullied. This might stop the bully in their tracks. It takes courage to make a stand.

Optional ending: "Until next time, this is _____ with Amazing Facts and Crazy Quizzes."

---

1. Dake, Price, Telljohaun, 2003

WEEK 13: DAY 4 (Crazy Quiz # 8)

"Hello, my name is _____ and this is Amazing Facts and Crazy Quizzes."

Take this quick quiz. If you are bullied who should you tell? A) your pet B) your mail carrier C) your parents. (Pause) The answer is C) your parents. It is also best to tell a teacher at school. Remember what TELL means: **T** stands for **T**alk clearly and plainly, **E** stands for **E**xplain what happen, the first **L** stands for **L**ist those involved and the last **L** stands for **L**isten to the adult's instructions.

Optional ending: "Until next time, this is _____ with Amazing Facts and Crazy Quizzes."

WEEK 13: DAY 5

"Hello, my name is _____ and this is Amazing Facts and Crazy Quizzes."

Research shows that bullying starts at home. Children learn how to be both a bully and a victim[1]. Negative parents hurt self-esteem and set a bad example. Mean brothers and sisters show how bulling works[2]. Children being picked on at home become life-long victims by losing their self-esteem[3]. Parents and children need to realize the importance of a safe and loving home. Stop bullying before it stops.

Optional ending: "Until next time, this is _____ with Amazing Facts and Crazy Quizzes."

---

1. Dake, Price, Telljohaun, 2003
2. Georgiou, Stavrinides, 2013
3. Lereya, Samara, Wolke, 2013

Tip for the Student Reader: Read the text beforehand and make sure you can pronounce each word correctly. Ask an adult for help if you come across a word that is difficult.

Notes:
_____
_____
_____
_____
_____
_____
_____

WEEK 14: DAY 1 (The Herd and the Hero)

"Hello, my name is _____ and this is Amazing Facts and Crazy Quizzes."

What does the word bystander mean to you? It refers to a person who is a witness of a bully attack. As a bystander, you can choose to be part of the herd and follow the bully. You could also choose to act like a hero instead. You can lend a hand to the victim and ask them to walk away with you. You could also stand up with others, stand by the victim, and halt the bully in his or her tracks. Speak calmly, but firmly and tell the person bullying to stop[1].

Optional ending: "Until next time, this is _____ with Amazing Facts and Crazy Quizzes."

---

1. Beane, 2014

WEEK 14: DAY 2 (Rule # 5 Review)

"Hello, my name is _____ and this is Amazing Facts and Crazy Quizzes."

Bullying is not an accident, but many "accidents" look like bullying. If someone is bothering you, do not assume he or she is trying to be mean. Use TALK to stop the problem. Find out what the other person is thinking. A brief conversation with the person will make it clear if it was an accident or not. Here is an amazing fact: we can stop accidents before they happen. Pay attention. Follow hallway rules, like do not run. Learn to take turns. Practice patience. All of these things can stop accidents and help everyone feel safe.

Optional ending: "Until next time, this is _____ with Amazing Facts and Crazy Quizzes."

WEEK 14: DAY 3 (Girls Bully Differently)

"Hello, my name is _____ and this is Amazing Facts and Crazy Quizzes."

One of the most terrible ways girls bully differently is with fake friendships. Buhle Belle pretends to be her target's friend and then turns against them. If you know a person like this, you need to realize that they do not care about you and are not your friend. Many people in school could be your best friend. Do not waste time with mean and cruel people[1]. You deserve good friends.

Optional ending: "Until next time, this is _____ with Amazing Facts and Crazy Quizzes."

---

1. Beane, 2014

WEEK 14: DAY 4

"Hello, my name is _____ and this is Amazing Facts and Crazy Quizzes."

   Bullies and **Bears** are alike in the way they treat other people. However, there are important differences. Bullies are often normal kids who do mean things. A person who is a Bear has had a very rough life. That makes them rough. Bullies target individuals. Bears could attack anyone, even teachers. A bully wants to control you. The Bear wants to hurt you physically. Know the difference and know how to handle yourself. Remember, you should use TWT with a bully, but not with a bear. If a person is acting like a Bear, walk away and report the bear immediately.

 Optional ending "Until next time, this is __ with Amazing Facts and Crazy Quizzes."

WEEK 14: DAY 5 (Crazy Quiz #9)

"Hello, my name is _____ and this is Amazing Facts and Crazy Quizzes."

   Her name is Nancy. Is she a bully or a Bear? Listen to the facts and decide. She picks on you every day. If you accidentally bump into her, she wants to fight. She yells at you if she feels you are looking at her. On her bad days, she is your worst nightmare. You notice that she acts just as mean to everyone else. Is she acting like a bully or is she acting like a Bear? (Pause) Here are the facts: Bullies pick on individual targets, not everyone, so this individual does not fit the rules of bullying. She is a Bear. A Bear is mean to everyone and thinks everyone is out to harm him or her. Many times, they come from a harsh background where aggression and rudeness is common, so this is how they react to accidents and everyday incidents.

Optional ending: "Until next time, this is __ with Amazing Facts and Crazy Quizzes."

[1]. National Crime Prevention Council, 2015

Tip for the Student Reader: The superscript numbers that look like this[1] refer to the references at the bottom of the page. These numbers[1] should not be read.

Notes:
_____
_____
_____
_____
_____
_____
_____

WEEK 15: DAY 1

"Hello, my name is _____ and this is Amazing Facts and Crazy Quizzes."

Meet Victor and Victoria. Victor and Victoria are ready to face problems at school. They have a positive self-image. They are full of energy and friendliness. They use TALK-WALK-TELL when someone is bothering them. They do not worry about what others think and say. Bullies figure out quickly that these two are not easy targets. They usually leave them alone[1]. Their names say it all. They are winners: Victor and Victoria.

Optional ending: "Until next time, this is _____ with Amazing Facts and Crazy Quizzes."

---

1. Lereya, Samara, Wolke, 2013

WEEK 15: DAY 2

"Hello, my name is _____ and this is Amazing Facts and Crazy Quizzes."

Adults often tell children to ignore problems as if this would make the problem go away. This strategy often causes undue anxiety and seldom works. In the case of the bully, it could be a serious mistake. Bullies want to control their targets. This means they want to force them to react to their taunts. Ignoring a bully will not make them go away. The bully is more likely to increase the aggression if he or she does not receive a response[1]. Use **TALK** to confront the problem in a calm manner and then use **WALK**. Remember, confidence will help you to be bully-proof.

Optional ending: "Until next time, this is _____ with Amazing Facts and Crazy Quizzes."

WEEK 15: DAY 3 (The Hero and the Herd)

"Hello, my name is _____ and this is Amazing Facts and Crazy Quizzes."

If you witness bullying, try to remember the details so you can report it to an adult. Use the strategy TELL to guide you: **T** is for **T**alk plainly and clearly, **E** is for **E**xplain what happened. The first **L** stands for **L**ist only those involved and the last **L** is for **L**isten to the advice the adult gives you. Dr. Beane from www.bullyfree.com suggests you write down the facts and include what happened before and after the bullying[1].

Optional ending: "Until next time, this is _____ with Amazing Facts and Crazy Quizzes."

---

1. Field, 1996

WEEK 15: DAY 4

"Hello, my name is _____ and this is Amazing Facts and Crazy Quizzes."

Why do students keep bullying a secret? Studies show that students are sometimes afraid to report bullying. They are embarrassed that they cannot stand up for themselves. This is more so if their parents expect them to do so[1]. Remember, everyone needs help some times. Also, remember this is not your fault. Report the bullying to a trusted adult who can help you. Teachers and staff can also help with talking to parents if needed[1].

Optional ending: "Until next time, this is _____ with Amazing Facts and Crazy Quizzes."

WEEK 15: DAY 5

"Hello, my name is _____ and this is Amazing Facts and Crazy Quizzes."

TALK, WALK, and TELL helps in most situations. The reason TALK is so important is that it is part of being assertive. Being assertive means to tell someone how you feel or think in a calm and confident manner. Being assertive is not being mean or aggressive. If you learn to use the strategy TALK, you will have less stress and solve more problems before they become too big to handle.

Optional ending: "Until next time, this is _____ with Amazing Facts and Crazy Quizzes."

---

1. Beane, 2014

Tip for the Student Reader: A web address is read differently than a sentence. www.stopbulling.gov/kid is w.w.w. Stop-bullying (dot) gov (forward slash) kid.

Notes:
_____
_____
_____
_____
_____
_____
_____

WEEK 16: DAY 1

"Hello, my name is _____ and this is Amazing Facts and Crazy Quizzes."

Bullies and Bears may look similar, but remember the differences. A bully will probably leave you alone if you show that you are not afraid and use TALK. A Bear, however, will probably punch you in the nose if you use TALK on them. Instead, use WALK and TELL when you know the aggressor is a Bear. Report the Bear immediately, he or she may be a danger to all students.

Optional ending: "Until next time, this is _____ with Amazing Facts and Crazy Quizzes."

WEEK 16: DAY 2

"Hello, my name is _____ and this is Amazing Facts and Crazy Quizzes."

A **perpetual victim** is a person who remains a target of bullying throughout their life[1]. In this case, the perpetual victim needs to start changing the way they look at things and take responsibility for the way they act and think[2]. Ask your school counselor or teacher how you can bully-proof yourself. You can also go online to www.stopbullying.com/kids to find out more.

Optional ending: "Until next time, this is _____ with Amazing Facts and Crazy Quizzes."

WEEK 16: DAY 3

"Hello, my name is _____ and this is Amazing Facts and Crazy Quizzes."

If it is not bullying, then what do you call it? The Bear has a different attitude than a bully. Bullies are very sneaky, but Bears are mean in broad daylight. Because of their backgrounds, they think everyone is out to get them so they are ready to throw the first punch. Do not try to use TALK on a Bear. Walk away if you can and report them to an adult.

Optional ending: "Until next time, this is _____ with Amazing Facts and Crazy Quizzes."

---

1. Elliott, 1993
2. Mathews, 2007

WEEK 16: DAY 4

"Hello, my name is _____ and this is Amazing Facts and Crazy Quizzes."

It is possible that you could punch the bully in the nose to make them quit calling you names. Of course, this could cause you to ruin your reputation, lose friends who do not like to hang with violent people, make other students afraid of you, and/or receive a strict consequence from the school, which could include out of school suspension. There are many non-violent ways to stop bullying. Fighting should never be the answer when you are at school. Sometimes parents tell their child to hit back. This is not the answer. This is the first step to becoming a bully yourself.

Optional ending: "Until next time, this is _____ with Amazing Facts and Crazy Quizzes."

WEEK 16: DAY 5 (Crazy Quiz #10)

"Hello, my name is _____ and this is Amazing Facts and Crazy Quizzes."

You walk the same way to the bus line every day and "she" is always standing there at the corner waiting for you. Angie is so prim and proper. She always has new shoes and pretty dresses. As soon as she sees you coming, she starts shaking her head and making that look on her face to show her disapproval of what you are wearing. She blurts as you walk by, "Those pants look like last week's rejects." (Pause) Is Angie a bully? (Pause) Yes, Angie fits the rules of bullying. Bullies are a constant problem. The best way to stop bullying is to use TWT, and report them to your teachers and parents.

Optional ending: "Until next time, this is _____ with Amazing Facts and Crazy Quizzes."

Tip for the Student Reader: Do not say the word (Pause) in a parenthesis. It is a direction for you to give a short break to let the audience think before you reveal the answer.

Notes:
_____
_____
_____
_____
_____
_____
_____

WEEK 17: DAY 1 (Crazy Quiz #11)

"Hello, my name is _____ and this is **Amazing Facts and Crazy Quizzes.**"

True or False - Buhle Bell is most likely to pick on her target by gathering a herd around her. The herd will help her taunt and tease them. (Pause) The answer is true, female bullies like to work in groups[1]. However, Buhle Bell is not afraid to go one on one when picking on others. When dealing with a herd or an individual bully use TALK-WALK-TELL. The key is to control your emotions.

Optional ending: "Until next time, this is _____ with Amazing Facts and Crazy Quizzes."

---

1. National Crime Prevention Council, 2015

WEEK 17: DAY 2

"Hello, my name is _____ and this is Amazing Facts and Crazy Quizzes."

Girls Bully Differently: What do you call a group of bullies? It would be accurate to call them a gang, but if they are bullies, maybe the name **herd** hits closer to home. Buhle Belle likes to recruit other girls to join her as she taunts and picks on her victim[1]. What self-respecting girl or boy would want to be a part of a herd? Do not allow the bully to be your ringleader.

Optional ending: "Until next time, this is _____ with Amazing Facts and Crazy Quizzes."

WEEK 17: DAY 3

"Hello, my name is _____ and this is Amazing Facts and Crazy Quizzes."

Dr. Alan Beane says to use positive self-talk when having a bully problem. Say something positive to yourself when a bully is trying to cut you down. This may help prevent the bully from making you feel bad. Positive self-talk is important when dealing with bullying[2].

Optional ending: "Until next time, this is _____ with Amazing Facts and Crazy Quizzes."

---

1. National Crime Prevention Council, 2015
2. Beane, 2014

WEEK 17: DAY 4 (The Hero and the Herd)

"Hello, my name is _____ and this is Amazing Facts and Crazy Quizzes."

Sometimes bystanders experience feelings of guilt, especially when they do not try to help the target. Speak to an adult about what happened. Tell them how you feel. No one is perfect. All of us can learn more about being bully-free. Talk to friends about what you all can do if there is bullying. Have a plan ahead of time so you and your friends will know what to do. Remember, it is not okay to be mean to the bully. Standing up together should be enough to stop them. Report the problem to an adult afterwards.

Optional ending: "Until next time, this is _____ with Amazing Facts and Crazy Quizzes."

WEEK 17: DAY 5 (Bully Proof)

"Hello, my name is _____ and this is Amazing Facts and Crazy Quizzes."

Some students are bully proof, like Victor and Victoria. They are characters from the Usual Suspects. They show confidence, good character and a great sense of humor. They know that people are going to say and do things that they do not like. They are ready because they have positive self-esteem and know how to use TALK-WALK-TELL. You can be like these two. Talk to your school counselor or parents. Ask them how you can be bully-proof.

Tip for the Student Reader: The superscript numbers that look like this[1] refer to the references at the bottom of the page. These numbers[1] should not be read.

Notes:
_____
_____
_____
_____
_____
_____
_____

WEEK 18: DAY 1

"Hello, my name is _____ and this is Amazing Facts and Crazy Quizzes."

If it is not bullying, then what do you call it? Meet the Bigfoot. Sometimes it looks like bullying, but important points are missing. For instance, Bigfoot may plow you over and knock you down. He or she is not trying to be mean. They are uncoordinated or clumsy. Sometimes they do not pay attention. You should still speak to them about what they are doing. Call them by name. Tell them what they did. Ask for a solution. We know that a student who acts like a Bigfoot is not doing it on purpose. However, everyone is responsible for his or her own actions and accidents. If they continue, report them to your teacher.

Optional ending: "Until next time, this is _____ with Amazing Facts and Crazy Quizzes."

WEEK 18: DAY 2

"Hello, my name is _____ and this is Amazing Facts and Crazy Quizzes."

Not every bothersome behavior is bullying. Remember the five rules of bullying. Bullies target their victims. Bullying is on purpose. It is repeated over and over again. It is unwanted aggression. It is meant to do harm. There is an imbalance of power. Do not use the term "bully" unless it fits the definition. Knowledge is power. Learn as much as you can about bullies and the other behaviors.

Optional ending: "Until next time, this is _____ with Amazing Facts and Crazy Quizzes."

WEEK 18: DAY 3

"Hello, my name is _____ and this is Amazing Facts and Crazy Quizzes."

The term "imbalance of power" is a big idea. It means that the person who is being picked on feels like they cannot defend themselves. One reason they feel this way is because they think the bully is right about what they are saying. For example, Brandi Brat is great at math. She is nagging on Suzy Q because she made a "C" on the last report card. Suzy does not argue about it and she does not tell the teacher because she knows that she is not good at math. She is embarrassed and afraid others will find out, so she suffers in silence. Brandi Brat is using her good grades as power over her target. Remember, everyone has talents and everyone has weaknesses. Love yourself as you are, but always try to do be your personal best.

Optional ending: "Until next time, this is _____ with Amazing Facts and Crazy Quizzes."

WEEK 18: DAY 4

"Hello, my name is _____ and this is Amazing Facts and Crazy Quizzes."

Bullies pick on individuals they think will not try to defend themselves[1]. When a target uses a strategy like TALK-WALK-TELL, the bully realizes that this person is not going to be a victim. They will probably move on. Strategies only work when they are used. Practice being assertive and using your words when a bully bothers you.

Optional ending: "Until next time, this is _____ with Amazing Facts and Crazy Quizzes."

WEEK 18: DAY 5 (Where Do Bullies Come From?)

"Hello, my name is _____ and this is Amazing Facts and Crazy Quizzes."

Bullies are not born, they are made. Think about this: the person bullying you is either being bullied by someone else or has been recently. Bullies make bullies. That means if you do not deal with your bully problem, you might continue the cycle and bully someone else. Talk to your parents or a trusted adult about how you feel and how you can stop the cycle of bullying.

Optional ending: "Until next time, this is _____ with Amazing Facts and Crazy Quizzes."

---

[1]. Anderson, Swiatowy, 2008

Tip for the Student Reader: If you want to be the very best spokesperson, ask someone you trust to listen to you read and ask them if they understand you.

Notes:
_____
_____
_____
_____
_____
_____
_____

WEEK 19: DAY 1

"Hello, my name is _____ and this is Amazing Facts and Crazy Quizzes."

If it is not bullying, then what do you call it? Bigfoot is one of the Usual Suspects. He or she may be going through a growth spurt and they are a little clumsy. Use TALK when a person is bothering you. Call them by name, tell them what they are doing that bothers you and ask for a solution. A Bigfoot probably does not know what he or she is doing. They need you to point out what it is so the activity can stop.

Optional ending: "Until next time, this is _____ with Amazing Facts and Crazy Quizzes."

WEEK 19: DAY 2

"Hello, my name is _____ and this is Amazing Facts and Crazy Quizzes."

Research shows that bullying might stop if bystanders would just step up and help the victim. In a study of Toronto elementary schools, researchers discovered that when a bystander told the bully to stop or asked the victim to leave with them, the bullying stopped fifty-seven percent of the time[1]. That means it worked more times than it did not. Stopbullying.gov says, "Make a stand. Lend a hand[2]."

Optional ending: "Until next time, this is _____ with Amazing Facts and Crazy Quizzes."

WEEK 19: DAY 3

"Hello, my name is _____ and this is Amazing Facts and Crazy Quizzes."

Victor and Victoria show their confidence by good posture. They walk with their heads up and their shoulders back. They are alert. They know what is going on around them. Bullies like to target individuals who do not pay attention. They like to pick on students who are shy and alone. When a person is happy and confident, bullies stay away. Stay tuned for more ways you can become bully-proof.

Optional ending: "Until next time, this is _____ with Amazing Facts and Crazy Quizzes."

---

[1]. Dake, Price, Telljohaun 2003, the Toronto Study
[2]. Stopbullying.gov | Bystander, 2014

WEEK 19: DAY 4

"Hello, my name is _____ and this is Amazing Facts and Crazy Quizzes."

A good way to be bully-proof is to show everyone that you are not a victim. Use good posture. Make eye contact with others. Be friendly. Remember Bully Boy and Bully Belle want an easy target and do not like to pick on people they cannot control[1]. Do not get mad, sad, or angry when someone picks on you. Ask them to stop and walk away.

Optional ending: "Until next time, this is _____ with Amazing Facts and Crazy Quizzes."

WEEK 19: DAY 5

"Hello, my name is _____ and this is Amazing Facts and Crazy Quizzes."

If it is not bullying, then what do you call it? Meet the Badger. He or she is targeting you. They are poking, pushing, pulling, and maybe even licking you. It may seem that they are a bully, but they do not mean to do you harm. They want to be your friend. Badger has poor social skills and needs someone to show him or her how to be a friend. Use TALK and explain to them that they are not being a good friend. If you find it in your heart, you could help them learn the skills they need.

Optional ending: "Until next time, this is _____ with Amazing Facts and Crazy Quizzes."

---

1. Kaiser, Rasminsky, *2009*

Tip for the Student Reader: As you read a Crazy Quiz make sure to say the letters for each choice. A) = A. B) = B. This will help the listener stay on track. Remember, do not read the (Pause) out loud.

Notes:
_____
_____
_____
_____
_____
_____
_____

WEEK 20: DAY 1 (Crazy Quiz #12)

"Hello, my name is _____ and this is Amazing Facts and Crazy Quizzes."

When a person says something to you that is rude or mean what is the best way to respond? A) punch them in the nose B) make fun of their ears C) remain calm and try to ignore them D) act assertive and ask the person to stop (Pause) The answer is D: act assertive, and ask the person to stop.

Remember that being assertive is not the same as being rude or bossy. Assertiveness is calmly expressing your thoughts, feelings, and wants. In this case using TALK would be the best way to handle the situation.

Optional ending: "Until next time, this is _____ with Amazing Facts and Crazy Quizzes."

WEEK 20: DAY 2 (Crazy Quiz #13)

"Hello, my name is _____ and this is Amazing Facts and Crazy Quizzes."

How long has bullying and other mean behaviors been around? What is the answer? A) It is a new thing. It just started when you came to elementary school. B) It has only been around since the news started reporting it. C) It has been a problem ever since there were two people in the same area. (Pause) The answer is C) Bullying is not new. You are not the only person who has ever had a person be mean to them. Recorded history refers to bullying thousands of years ago.

Optional ending: "Until next time, this is _____ with Amazing Facts and Crazy Quizzes."

WEEK 20: DAY 3

"Hello, my name is _____ and this is Amazing Facts and Crazy Quizzes."

Some adults think they can spot a bully from a mile away. The amazing fact is: no one can tell who is a bully just be looking at him or her. Bullying is an action. There are no outward signs until it happens. Bullies do not wear certain clothes. They do not have a particular posture. Bullies do not have mean facial expressions. They are normal students who look and act like everyone else, until they see their target and start the act of bullying.

Optional ending: "Until next time, this is _____ with Amazing Facts and Crazy Quizzes."

WEEK 20: DAY 4 (Crazy Quiz # 14)

"Hello, my name is _____ and this is Amazing Facts and Crazy Quizzes."

Are you a Victor or victim? Take this quiz to see how close you are to being the next bully victim. Do you like to daydream? Do you like to be alone? Do you feel like you are not very good at making friends? Do you cry or become upset easily? If you answered "YES" to most or all of these questions, then you are in danger of being the next bully victim. Do not wait until it is too late! Contact your school counselor for help.

Optional ending: "Until next time, this is _____ with Amazing Facts and Crazy Quizzes."

WEEK 20: DAY 5

"Hello, my name is _____ and this is Amazing Facts and Crazy Quizzes."

Is it bullying? Here are the clues. Sarah and Misty do not like each other. They have been mean to each other since kindergarten. Sarah calls Misty names. Misty spreads rumors about Sarah. Both stare and hiss at each other when they walk by. (Pause) Which one is the bully? This is a case where two individuals, with equal power and an equal amount of guilt, are competing with each other over who can be the meanest. Neither person is a bully, but both of them are mean, rude and need a trip to the principal's office! The Usual Suspects call them Bucky and Becca Buckette.

Optional ending: "Until next time, this is _____ with Amazing Facts and Crazy Quizzes."

Tip for the Student Reader: Respect the punctuation. Periods (.) are like a stop sign. Take a short break at each period. You might take a breath at the period. Keeping the sentences separated by a short break helps keep the meaning clear.

Notes:
_____
_____
_____
_____
_____
_____
_____

WEEK 21: DAY 1

"Hello, my name is _____ and this is Amazing Facts and Crazy Quizzes."

If it is not bullying, then what do you call it? The Usual Suspects calls it being a Badger. This is when a person lacks the social skills to recognize the cues that they are bugging you. Billy Badger wants to be your friend but if you do not TALK to him, he may become your worst nightmare. It is ok to tell others you do not like how they are playing. Suggest something new or show them how to play like a friend.

Optional ending: "Until next time, this is _____ with Amazing Facts and Crazy Quizzes."

WEEK 21: DAY 2

"Hello, my name is _____ and this is Amazing Facts and Crazy Quizzes."

Research shows three ways bully-victims are made. In a study by professor Wolke, victims are created by parents and siblings. First, by parents who are constantly critical and harsh, and secondly, by parents who are over protective. Thirdly, victims are molded by their brothers and sisters who bully them at home[1]. Home should be a happy place. Talk to your parents about the amazing facts you learn.

Optional ending: "Until next time, this is _____ with Amazing Facts and Crazy Quizzes."

WEEK 21: DAY 3

"Hello, my name is _____ and this is Amazing Facts and Crazy Quizzes."

Cyberbullying is when bullying happens online[1]. It happens in places like chat rooms, Facebook, and Instagram. It also happens during online video games. The answer to preventing cyberbullying for kids is easy. Stay off these social media sites. They are for adults! Go outside and play. Read a book, or play a board game with your friends and family. If you want to talk to friends, use your phone. Do not call or text people who are mean to you.

Optional ending: "Until next time, this is _____ with Amazing Facts and Crazy Quizzes."

---

1. Lereya, Samara, Wolke, 2013

WEEK 21: DAY 4

"Hello, my name is _____ and this is Amazing Facts and Crazy Quizzes."

Do not take the bully so seriously. Yes, they are serious when they try to make fun of your nose or ears. Why should you care about what he or she thinks? If you like yourself, bullies cannot hurt you with their hateful and untrue words.

Optional ending: "Until next time, this is _____ with Amazing Facts and Crazy Quizzes."

WEEK 21: DAY 5 (Crazy Quiz #15)

"Hello, my name is _____ and this is Amazing Facts and Crazy Quizzes."

Which Usual Suspect is described by the following story? Here are the clues. He or she may be called a bully because they bump into people a lot. This suspect does not intend to do harm, but it sure does hurt when they accidentally step on your toes or poke you with their elbow as they walk by. (Pause) Which Usual Suspect do you think it is? A) Billy Badger 2) Buhle Belle 3) Bigfoot? (Pause) The answer is Bigfoot. A Bigfoot is often careless and accident-prone. The amazing fact is while his or her actions are a mistake, it is important to realize that it is everyone's responsibility to be careful and kind.

Optional ending: "Until next time, this is _____ with Amazing Facts and Crazy Quizzes."

1. Stopbullying.gov | cyberbullying, 2014

Tip for the Student Reader: Changing the pitch or tone of your voice makes it easier to listen to your reading. This is called inflection in your voice. Ask a sponsor or perhaps your music teacher to help you with this.

Notes:
_____
_____
_____
_____
_____
_____
_____

WEEK 22: DAY 1

"Hello, my name is _____ and this is Amazing Facts and Crazy Quizzes."

If it is not bullying, then what do you call it? Meet the Buck. Buck love to play sports and he or she thinks everyone loves to play rough like he does. Use TALK to explain that you are not interested in rough-housing. If he or she does not stop WALK away. As always, if the Buck does not "get it," then you may need to TELL an adult.

Optional ending: "Until next time, this is _____ with Amazing Facts and Crazy Quizzes."

WEEK 22: DAY 2

"Hello, my name is _____ and this is Amazing Facts and Crazy Quizzes."

Why do some students keep bullying a secret? Sometimes students do not want their parents to worry[1]. There is a better way to think about this situation. If your parents know that you can deal with problems by reporting them, they will be able to spend less time worrying about you. Use TALK, WALK and TELL to handle conflicts. Your parents will be glad you did.

Optional ending: "Until next time, this is _____ with Amazing Facts and Crazy Quizzes."

WEEK 22: DAY 3

"Hello, my name is _____ and this is Amazing Facts and Crazy Quizzes."

The hero and the herd. Bullies love an audience. As a bystander, do not stand by and watch[2]. If you do not feel you can stand up to the bully, walk away and find an adult to help.

Optional ending: "Until next time, this is _____ with Amazing Facts and Crazy Quizzes."

---

1. Beane, 2014
2. www.Stopbullying.gov | Bystander, 2014

WEEK 22: DAY 4

"Hello, my name is _____ and this is Amazing Facts and Crazy Quizzes."

Bullies may be a boy or girl, tall or short, younger or older, bigger or smaller, thin and cute or plain and plump. Anyone could be a bully if he or she does not watch his or her words and actions. Stop bullying from the inside out. Decide right now to be a buddy not a bully.

Optional ending: "Until next time, this is _____ with Amazing Facts and Crazy Quizzes."

WEEK 22: DAY 5

"Hello, my name is _____ and this is Amazing Facts and Crazy Quizzes."

An old proverb says that a friend is sometimes better to you than a brother is[1]. Research shows that in many cases bullying starts in the home[2]. It starts with brothers or sisters constantly pick on each other. One sibling may think nothing of it while another learns to be a bully or a victim[3]. When you know another student is having a hard time at home, try to be his or her friend. They need a buddy to help them forget about the bullies at home. You may stop that person from becoming a bully because of your friendship.

Optional ending: "Until next time, this is _____ with Amazing Facts and Crazy Quizzes."

---

1. Proverbs 18:24, the Bible
2. Lereya, Samara, Wolke, 2013
3. Georgiou, Stavrinides, 2013

Tip for the Student Reader: As you read a Crazy Quiz, make sure to say the letters for each choice. A) = A. B) = B. This will help the listener stay on track.

Notes:
_____
_____
_____
_____
_____
_____

WEEK 23: DAY 1 (Crazy Quiz #16)

"Hello, my name is _____ and this is Amazing Facts and Crazy Quizzes."

Which Usual Suspect could this be? Here are the clues. She tells you she is your friend and invites you to hang out with her inner circle. When you are comfortable with them, she turns on you and says terrible thing about you to her friends. After this, she spreads rumors and makes faces at you when you walk by. (Pause) A) Betty Badger B) Buhle Belle C) Bingo the Dingo. (Pause) The answer is B: Buhle Belle.

Optional ending: "Until next time, this is _____ with Amazing Facts and Crazy Quizzes."

WEEK 23: DAY 2

"Hello, my name is _____ and this is Amazing Facts and Crazy Quizzes."

If it is not bullying, then what do you call it? He or she likes to wrestle and play rough. They may love to trash talk at recess or in the gym. They do not live up to the rules of bulling so what do you call them? He or she is what the Usual Suspects call a Buck. Have you ever seen two bucks hitting heads in an open field? It is all about competition and roughhousing. Bucks needs to realize that most people do not like to play rough. In fact, it is against school rules to play fight or wrestle. Use TALK to explain that you do not like to play that way. You may also need to find someone else to play with.

Optional ending: "Until next time, this is _____ with Amazing Facts and Crazy Quizzes."

WEEK 23: DAY 3

"Hello, my name is _____ and this is Amazing Facts and Crazy Quizzes."

Rule #1 Review: If Bullies target their victims, why do they pick on that certain person. Most of the time the bully does not know why he or she picks on that person. Why do you think? Stay tuned to Amazing Facts and Crazy Quizzes for possible answers.

Optional ending: "Until next time, this is _____ with Amazing Facts and Crazy Quizzes."

WEEK 23: DAY 4 (The Hero and the Herd)

"Hello, my name is _____ and this is Amazing Facts and Crazy Quizzes."

Do not just stand there and watch the negative interaction. The bully wants an audience. Do not let him or her use you to mistreat the victim. One thing you could do is walk away and announce to everyone that you are going to tell a teacher. Our school needs heroes who will help stop bullying.

Optional ending: "Until next time, this is _____ with Amazing Facts and Crazy Quizzes."

WEEK 23: DAY 5

"Hello, my name is _____ and this is Amazing Facts and Crazy Quizzes."

Meet the Victim. Most experts agree that victims have common traits[1]. These include being a loner, having poor social skills and low self-esteem[2]. In the Usual Suspects, the character is Vic Victim. It is as if he has a bull's eye target on his back. It seems every bully want to pick on him. Listen up to Amazing Facts and Crazy Quizzes to learn more about Vic Victim.

Optional ending: "Until next time, this is _____ with Amazing Facts and Crazy Quizzes."

---

1. Elliott, 1993
2. Stopbullying.gov | Risk Factors, 2014

Tip for the Student Reader: Do not read the references at the bottom of the page.

Notes:
_____
_____
_____
_____
_____
_____
_____

WEEK 24: DAY 1 (If it is Not Bullying, What Do You Call it?)

"Hello, my name is _____ and this is Amazing Facts and Crazy Quizzes."

Meet Bingo and Blingo. He or she is a likeable person. They are probably good at a lot of things that are practical and helpful, but something happens that triggers a big change. Bingo and Blingo turn into wild dingoes! They are not good at math or writing and they will do anything to get out of classwork. Bingos should never get out of work because they act up. Instead, they need to learn to ask for help!

Optional ending: "Until next time, this is _____ with Amazing Facts and Crazy Quizzes."

WEEK 24: DAY 2 (Where do Bullies come from?)

"Hello, my name is _____ and this is Amazing Facts and Crazy Quizzes."

Bullies are not born. They are raised in negative homes and created by bothersome peers[1]. When children are bullied by relatives and others, they learn how to bully. When they see others who bully go unpunished, they are encouraged to use the same behavior[2]. Bullying starts on the inside and it can stop from the inside out. Think about how you treat others. Choose to be a hero!

Optional ending: "Until next time, this is _____ with Amazing Facts and Crazy Quizzes."

WEEK 24: DAY 3 (Crazy Quiz #17)

"Hello, my name is _____ and this is Amazing Facts and Crazy Quizzes."

Here are the clues. Which Usual Suspect is it? He is your friend and you have a great time playing during recess. You sit by each other in math class and everything seems to be going great. Suddenly your buddy starts acting grumpy and mean. He yells at you for touching his paper and then he knocks his desk over. (Pause) Your choices are. A) Bully Boy B) Dr. Jekyll and Mr. Hyde C) Bingo the Dingo. (Pause) The answer is C) Bingo the Dingo. If a person near you has a Dingo-fit, stay calm and stay out of the way.

Optional ending: "Until next time, this is _____ with Amazing Facts and Crazy Quizzes."

---

1. Georgiou, Stavrinides, 2013
2. Cohn & Canter, 2003

WEEK 24: DAY 4 (Why do Students Keep Bullying a Secret?)

"Hello, my name is _____ and this is Amazing Facts and Crazy Quizzes."

One reason that students do not report bullying is they do not think teachers will do anything about it. They have told adults before and nothing happened about it[1]. Many states have new laws that require teachers to take bully reports serious. Do not give up. If you have tried TALK and WALK and things are not better, it is time to use TELL. If your teacher does not do anything about it, report the problem to your school counselor or principal. Remember to tell your parents. This is too important to keep it to yourself.

Optional ending: "Until next time, this is _____ with Amazing Facts and Crazy Quizzes."

WEEK 24: DAY 5

"Hello, my name is _____ and this is Amazing Facts and Crazy Quizzes."

The word bully continues to be misused by parents and teachers. Many adults use the word even if the actions do not fit the rules[2]. In the Usual Suspects, a person who is quick to hit and push is described as Buster Bear. The bear has anger issues. They need serious help. Here are a few differences between Buster Bear and Bully Boy. Bully Boy picks on certain individuals. Buster Bear is potentially mean to everyone. Bully Boy wants to control his targets. Buster wants to hurt the people he attacks. It is impossible to identify a bully just by looking at them. A person acting like Buster Bear often wears a frown or looks grumpy.

Optional ending: "Until next time, this is _____ with Amazing Facts and Crazy Quizzes."

1. Beane, 2014,
2. Dake, Price, Telljohaun 2003

Tip for the Student Reader: Stand confident and speak loud and clear. You are sharing important information! Make sure your audience understands you.

Notes:
_____
_____
_____
_____
_____
_____
_____

WEEK 25: DAY 1

"Hello, my name is _____ and this is Amazing Facts and Crazy Quizzes."

Bullying on the Bus: Riding the bus could be a perfect place for bothersome behaviors. With assigned seating and no place to go, students on the bus must be smart. If a person is bothering you on the bus, use TALK. If the person is keeps being mean, report it to the bus driver and your parents. Contact school officials if it continues. Parents should request the problem to be resolved immediately. Parents should ask for the bully to be moved to another seat.

Optional ending: "Until next time, this is _____ with Amazing Facts and Crazy Quizzes."

WEEK 25: DAY 2

"Hello, my name is _____ and this is Amazing Facts and Crazy Quizzes."

How you treat your younger brother or sister is very important. It could determine if you become a bully at school[1]. Siblings can be irritating. When you decide to be mean to your brothers or sisters, you are preparing yourself to be a bully. You may also be training your younger brother or sister to be a victim[1]. Think about what you are doing and how it will affect you and your family. The home should be a place of safety and love. Practice being nice to your family.

Optional ending: "Until next time, this is _____ with Amazing Facts and Crazy Quizzes."

WEEK 25: DAY 3 (Why do Students Keep Bullying a Secret?)

"Hello, my name is _____ and this is Amazing Facts and Crazy Quizzes."

Dr. Allan Beane of www.bullyfree.com explains that students are told since kindergarten not to tattle tale. Sources say that this is one reason students choose not to report bullying[1]. Reporting a bully who has bothered you repeatedly is not tattling. It is a good thing to do.

Optional ending: "Until next time, this is _____ with Amazing Facts and Crazy Quizzes."

---

1. Beane, 2014

WEEK 25: DAY 4 (Crazy Quiz # 18)

"Hello, my name is _____ and this is Amazing Facts and Crazy Quizzes."

What is the best way to handle a Bear? You accidently bump into Buster Bear in the hall. He turns and threatens to "punch your lights out." What should you do?

A) Punch him first, B) Run away screaming, C) Say, "My bad" and WALK away.

The best answer is C. Tell him that you are sorry and walk away before he can start a fight or argument.

Optional ending: "Until next time, this is _____ with Amazing Facts and Crazy Quizzes."

WEEK 25: DAY 5

"Hello, my name is _____ and this is Amazing Facts and Crazy Quizzes."

Most bullies in elementary school act tough, but they usually do not want to fight. Bears, on the other hand, will be aggressive and attack without warning. Bucks are very competitive and may think fighting is a way to make friends or have fun. Two of these Usual Suspects will stop if you TALK to them. One of them cannot be reasoned with. He or she may become meaner if you try to be assertive. Which suspect should you walk away from as soon as possible? The Bully, the Bear, or the Buck. (Pause) The answer is the Bear.

1. Georgiou, Stavrinides, 2013

Tip for the Student Reader: Read the text beforehand and make sure you can pronounce each word correctly. Ask an adult for help if you come across a word that is difficult.

Notes:
_____
_____
_____
_____
_____
_____
_____

WEEK 26: DAY 1

"Hello, my name is _____ and this is Amazing Facts and Crazy Quizzes."

Physical bullying increases in elementary school, peaks in middle school and declines in high school. Verbal bullying like name-calling remains the same[1]. Stop bullying before it starts. Learn all you can about being bully-proof now to prepare for the upper grades. TALK-WALK-TELL can be used in all grades.

Optional ending: "Until next time, this is _____ with Amazing Facts and Crazy Quizzes."

---

1. Cohn & Canter, 2003

WEEK 26: DAY 2

"Hello, my name is _____ and this is Amazing Facts and Crazy Quizzes."

Those who bully are more likely to abuse alcohol and drugs when they are older[1]. The attitude and actions of the bully harms others. It also hurts themselves[2]. Save yourself a lot of trouble and stop bullying now!

Optional ending: "Until next time, this is _____ with Amazing Facts and Crazy Quizzes."

WEEK 26: DAY 3

"Hello, my name is _____ and this is Amazing Facts and Crazy Quizzes."

A person that acts like a Bear comes from an environment of violence. He or she has few positive roles models in their life. Without help, these students will tend to become gang members. They are also more likely to break the law when they become older[3].

Optional ending: "Until next time, this is _____ with Amazing Facts and Crazy Quizzes."

---

1. Stopbullying.gov | At-Risk, 2014
2. Juvonen, Wang, Espinoza, 2013
3. Seely, Tombari, Bennett and Dunkle, 2011.

WEEK 26: DAY 4

"Hello, my name is _____ and this is Amazing Facts and Crazy Quizzes."

Bullying increases in 6th, 7th, and 8th grades. It becomes more physical than verbal[1]. It is wise for students to have a plan before they hit the middle school arena. Learn TALK-WALK-TELL. Build strong friendships now. Agree to help each other during a crisis. Remember that bullies look for an easy target so learn the ways of the Victor and prepare yourself now.

Optional ending: "Until next time, this is _____ with Amazing Facts and Crazy Quizzes."

WEEK 26: DAY 5

"Hello, my name is _____ and this is Amazing Facts and Crazy Quizzes."

Bullying could happen anywhere and at any time. It is more likely to happen when there is not adult supervision like in the hallways and restrooms. It also happens in a place with a lack of structure such as at recess, or at lunch[2]. Be alert and be safe!

Optional ending: "Until next time, this is _____ with Amazing Facts and Crazy Quizzes."

---

1. Bullying: Facts for Schools and Parents, 2003
2. Beane, 2014

Note to the Student Reader: When you come across ____, you call them "blank." Example: Bullies (blank) their victims. After you repeat the question with the "blank," read the sentence with the answer.

Notes:
_____
_____
_____
_____
_____
_____
_____

WEEK 27: DAY 1

"Hello, my name is _____ and this is Amazing Facts and Crazy Quizzes."

Rule #2 Review: Bullying is a constant problem. The same person bothers you all of the time. When you see that person coming you think to yourself, "What are they going to do to me now?" Use TALK WALK and TELL or another strategy your school promotes. If the bullying has been going on for a long time, you will probably need an adult's help. Report the bullying to your school staff. Always tell your parents.

Optional ending: "Until next time, this is _____ with Amazing Facts and Crazy Quizzes."

WEEK 27: DAY 2

"Hello, my name is _____ and this is Amazing Facts and Crazy Quizzes."

Gossip is one way that bullies try to hurt their victims[1]. If a person tries to say something hurtful about another student, ask the gossiper to stop. Most of the time gossip is not true. It can still be very hurtful. Tell an adult you trust about the gossip and then keep it to yourself.

Optional ending: "Until next time, this is _____ with Amazing Facts and Crazy Quizzes."

WEEK 27: DAY 3

"Hello, my name is _____ and this is Amazing Facts and Crazy Quizzes."

What is a red cape? You have probably seen a cartoon of a matador flapping a red cape in front of a bull. The bull thinks the cape is a part of the person. He attacks the cape and not the matador. In bullying, a red cape is what a bully sees that makes him or her want to attack. A red cape could be anything that might remind the bully of his or her own bad experiences[2]. The targeted person needs to realize that the problem is with the bully. Bully Boy is wrong. No one has the right to be mean to others. Tell an adult at school and your parents.

---

1. Eder, 1991
2. McLeod, (2008)

WEEK 27: DAY 4

"Hello, my name is _____ and this is Amazing Facts and Crazy Quizzes."

Bullies want to make their victims mad, sad, or afraid. This makes them feel like they have power. Determine now that you will not give the bully what he or she wants. Do not let them see your negative emotions. Use Talk and then WALK away before you lose your cool.

WEEK 27: DAY 5 (Crazy Quiz #19)

"Hello, my name is _____ and this is Amazing Facts and Crazy Quizzes."

Who would make a better friend? Buhle Belle or Victoria? (Pause) The answer is easy. Buhle Belle will be mean and try to hurt your feelings. Victoria will be friendly and teach you positive habits. Choose your friends wisely[2]. Know the difference between a buddy and a bully.

1. Juvonen, Wang, Espinoza, 2013

A Note to the Student Reader: Amazing Facts is a very important part of the day. Read the text beforehand and make sure you can pronounce each word correctly. Ask an adult for help if you come across a word that is difficult.

Notes:
_____
_____
_____
_____
_____
_____
_____

WEEK 28: DAY 1

"Hello, my name is _____ and this is Amazing Facts and Crazy Quizzes."

Tag you are it. That is, you are now the bully! Playing tag is a fun game. Some schools, however, have crossed it off the list of games students can play at recess. Many times students are hurt because they are "tagged" in the face. They also fall as someone tries to tag them. Another reason the game is prohibited in many schools is because the word bully is used too often. Children often forget that they were willingly playing the game when they were hurt. They want to call the other student a bully or report him or her to the teachers. Bullying is not an accident and accidents are not bullying. If you are hurt while playing a game, you need to own up to the fact that it is an accident and stop acting like a victim. Who knows, if you keep complaining, your school may take the game "tag" off the list of games you can play.

Optional ending: "Until next time, this is _____ with Amazing Facts and Crazy Quizzes."

WEEK 28: DAY 2 (The Hero and the Herd)

"Hello, my name is _____ and this is Amazing Facts and Crazy Quizzes."

Do not stand by and watch a bully mistreat others. The bully wants an audience. Instead, give him a posse to deal with. One thing you can do is stand beside the victim and ask the bully to stop. Talk to your buddies ahead of time and agree to stand up together if you see bullying take place[1]. Remember, you should not threaten the bully with violence. Be a champion, not a chump.

Optional ending: "Until next time, this is _____ with Amazing Facts and Crazy Quizzes."

WEEK 28: DAY 3

"Hello, my name is _____ and this is Amazing Facts and Crazy Quizzes."

Do you know the difference between a bully and a Badger? Sometimes they look the same, but there are a lot of differences. A bully wants to harm you. Billy and Becca Badger want to be your friend. The bully wants to make you sad or mad, but the Badger wants to make you happy. Billy and Becca lack positive social skills and do not realize that they are bothering you. They may push, pull, and poke you as their way of being friendly. Use TALK to let him or her know that you do not like what they are doing. If you have it in your heart to be a real hero, you could help the badger learn how to be a friend with patience, kindness, and good advice.

Optional ending: "Until next time, this is _____ with Amazing Facts and Crazy Quizzes."

---

1. Stopbullying.gov | Bystander, 2014

WEEK 28: DAY 4 (Crazy Quiz #20)

"Hello, my name is _____ and this is Amazing Facts and Crazy Quizzes."

Listen to this case and decide if it describes a Bully, Bear or Badger. Wilson is quiet, but he has been doing strange things lately. He sits at your table at lunch and tosses his food at you. Sometimes he asks you if you want a bite of his half-eaten apple. You think it is nasty, but he acts as if he is being your best friend when he does this. (Pause) So, which is it, Bully, Bear or Badger? (Pause) Wilson is acting like a Badger. Use TALK to help Wilson understand how to be a friend and not a fiend.

Optional ending: "Until next time, this is _____ with Amazing Facts and Crazy Quizzes."

WEEK 28: DAY 5

"Hello, my name is _____ and this is Amazing Facts and Crazy Quizzes."

What does a bully look like? You should know by now that a bully does not have a special look. Just because a person might be mad or sad does not mean they will turn into a Bully Boy and start picking on someone. A bully looks like a normal person because they are a normal person. When a person is a bully, you will see it in their words and actions, not in how they physically look.

Optional ending: "Until next time, this is _____ with Amazing Facts and Crazy Quizzes."

One more note to the student reader: As you read Amazing Facts and Crazy Quizzes, use the pitch or tone in your voice to help others understand what you are saying. Ask a sponsor to help you with this.

Notes:
_____
_____
_____
_____
_____
_____
_____

WEEK 29: DAY 1

"Hello, my name is _____ and this is Amazing Facts and Crazy Quizzes."

Review of WALK: If you are reading a book and a bully picks on you, use TALK to show the bully that you are not an easy target. Then WALK away. The **W** stands for **W**alk do not run (running shows you are afraid and the bully might chase you). **A** stands for **A**way from the problem (going a few feet away from the bully will not work). **L** stands for **L**ooking for a safe place to continue what you were doing (you should not have to stop reading because a bully interrupts you). Find a safe place near an adult or group of friends and continue to read. The **K** stands for **K**eep your cool (you need to think and pay attention to stay safe).

Optional ending: "Until next time, this is _____ with Amazing Facts and Crazy Quizzes."

WEEK 29: DAY 2

"Hello, my name is _____ and this is Amazing Facts and Crazy Quizzes."

Remember what TALK is about: Talk to the person bothering you- Call them by name- Tell them what they are doing that bothers you- Ask for a solution. It is not good enough to know how to use TALK; it will do you no good unless you use it when you need it. Use it when a friend is bothering you. Use it when a bully is picking on you. Use TALK when a brother or sister is doing something you do not like. Remember, others may use TWT on you. Plan to respond in a positive manner.

Optional ending: "Until next time, this is _____ with Amazing Facts and Crazy Quizzes."

WEEK 29: DAY 3

"Hello, my name is _____ and this is Amazing Facts and Crazy Quizzes."

There are different kinds of bullies. Most students who bully want to be mean and control their targets. Sometimes, especially in higher grades, some want to beat up their victims. Many experts say, however, that a bully is more like a coward than a tough fighter. When the victim starts to show a backbone, they back off[1].

Optional ending: "Until next time, this is _____ with Amazing Facts and Crazy Quizzes."

---

1. Bullying: Facts for Schools and Parents, 2003

WEEK 29: DAY 4 (Crazy Quiz # 21)

"Hello, my name is _____ and this is Amazing Facts and Crazy Quizzes."

Are you a Victor or victim? Take this quiz to see how close you are to being the next bully victim. Do you pay attention? Do you have friends you play with on the playground? Do you know who to talk to if someone is bothering you? If you answered "YES" to all of the above, you are on your way to be a VICTOR (or Victoria) and not a victim. Use your skills to be safe and use TALK, WALK and TELL to handle your problems.

Optional ending: "Until next time, this is _____ with Amazing Facts and Crazy Quizzes."

WEEK 29: DAY 5

"Hello, my name is _____ and this is Amazing Facts and Crazy Quizzes."

Verbal bullying is the most widespread type of bullying. Physical bullying occurs more in middle school. Cyberbullying takes place more in high school[1]. Knowledge is power. Learn to be bully-proof now and prepare for the future. You do not have to wait for adults to tell you. Talk to your school counselor. Read more about the Usual Suspects. Use the many anti-bully websites to learn the facts.

Optional ending: "Until next time, this is _____ with Amazing Facts and Crazy Quizzes."

A Note to the Student Reader: Amazing Facts is a very important part of the day. Read the text beforehand and make sure you can pronounce each word correctly.

Notes:
_____
_____
_____
_____
_____
_____
_____

WEEK 30: DAY 1

"Hello, my name is _____ and this is Amazing Facts and Crazy Quizzes."

Stop bullying from the inside out. Listen to yourself! You are patient and kind to just about everyone, but there is that one person you are always mean to every time you see them. Do they remind you of someone who used to bully you? Do they remind you of something about yourself that you do not like? It really does not matter; stop the bullying from the inside out. Decide today to stop what you are doing and ask the person to forgive you. They might a better friend than target.

Optional ending: "Until next time, this is _____ with Amazing Facts and Crazy Quizzes."

WEEK 30: DAY 2

"Hello, my name is _____ and this is Amazing Facts and Crazy Quizzes."

According to surveys, at least 10% of school-aged children feel bullied on a regular basis[1]. In a school that has 700 students, how many students experience bullying on a regular basis? Can you do the math? Ten percent of 700 is... (Pause) The answer is 70. Seventy students are experiencing bullying in a school of 700. Other studies show the percentage to be even higher. Report the problem to your teacher, principal and your parents. Keep use TELL until an adult helps and the problem is solved.

Optional ending: "Until next time, this is _____ with Amazing Facts and Crazy Quizzes."

WEEK 30: DAY 3

"Hello, my name is _____ and this is Amazing Facts and Crazy Quizzes."

Perpetual bullies are four times more likely to have three or more criminal convictions by age 24[2]. Each time you bully you are becoming more like a criminal. Decide now to stop bullying from the inside out. It all starts in you! The amazing fact is: even in elementary school, you are responsible for the choices you make.

Optional ending: "Until next time, this is _____ with Amazing Facts and Crazy Quizzes."

---

1. Bullying, "Facts for Families," No. 80 (3/11)
2. Understanding School Violence, 2013

WEEK 30: DAY 4

"Hello, my name is _____ and this is Amazing Facts and Crazy Quizzes."

If a person uses any kind of weapon to bully it becomes a serious crime. It is illegal to bring a knife, gun, or other kinds of weapons to school*. The student will face serious consequences. If a weapon is discovered on campus, it is possible that the school will call the police and press charges[1]. There are better ways to protect yourself against bullies. Learn to use TALK-WALK-TELL. Practice reporting only serious problems to your teacher. If you are known as a person who tattle-tells, teachers may not listen. Always talk to your parents about problems like this.

Optional ending: "Until next time, this is _____ with Amazing Facts and Crazy Quizzes."

WEEK 30: DAY 5

"Hello, my name is _____ and this is Amazing Facts and Crazy Quizzes."

Victor and Victoria are bully-proof. That means that they are less likely to be bothered by a bully. If Bully Boy tries to pick on them, they know to stay calm and use TALK-WALK-TELL to show that they are assertive, and not an easy target. Practice using this strategy with friends. Be prepared and be ready.

Optional ending: "Until next time, this is _____ with Amazing Facts and Crazy Quizzes."

---

*A Note to Administration (Do not read during announcements.) Make sure you understand your district policies. The district police will know how to handle the situations and will be a great resource for campus security.

1. Stopbullying.gov | Stop Bullying on the Spot, 2014

Yet Another Note to the Student Reader: Sometimes you will come to the word (Pause) in a parenthesis. Do not say the word out loud. It is a direction for you to give a short break before you continue. This will give the audience time to think of the answer before you reveal it.

Optional ending: "Until next time, this is _____ with Amazing Facts and Crazy Quizzes."

Notes:
_____
_____
_____
_____
_____
_____
_____

WEEK 31: DAY 1

"Hello, my name is _____ and this is Amazing Facts and Crazy Quizzes."

Empathy is the ability to recognize and share how others feel. A healthy child sees tears and feels pity or compassion. Bullies, on the other hand, just do not care how others feel. They are self-centered and selfish. A person who bullies repeatedly may lack empathy. Empathy is the ability to know how others feel. If you have a friend that bullies do not put up with it. Tell them to stop immediately. Try to help them understand how others feel. If they continue to bully, you may need to stop hanging around them.

Optional ending: "Until next time, this is _____ with Amazing Facts and Crazy Quizzes."

WEEK 31: DAY 2 (Crazy Quiz # 22)

"Hello, my name is _____ and this is Amazing Facts and Crazy Quizzes."

Is it bullying or something else? Two boys fight each other on the playground because they had a problem during a basketball game. Is this bullying? (Pause) The answer is no. This is against the rules. It is dangerous. It is wrong! Both students may be suspended from school, but it does not follow the rules of bullying. Know the rules of bullying and know the rules at school.

Optional ending: "Until next time, this is _____ with Amazing Facts and Crazy Quizzes."

WEEK 31: DAY 3

"Hello, my name is _____ and this is Amazing Facts and Crazy Quizzes."

What do you do if a student tells you that a bully is picking on them? If you are a teacher, you must take it seriously. Many school districts have passed regulations that require staff to act upon the report immediately. Separate the bully and target. Make sure everyone is safe. Record the information available. You do not have to investigate the incident, but you do have to report the incident to an administrator or school counselor[1].

Optional ending: "Until next time, this is _____ with Amazing Facts and Crazy Quizzes."

---

1. Stopbullying.gov | Stop Bullying on the Spot, 2014

WEEK 31: DAY 4

"Hello, my name is _____ and this is Amazing Facts and Crazy Quizzes."

A person's reputation is very important. A reputation is how others think of you. Do the kids at school think of you as a troublemaker or a peacekeeper? How do the teachers think of you? It is all up to you. It is your attitude and actions that make or break your reputation.

Optional ending: "Until next time, this is _____ with Amazing Facts and Crazy Quizzes."

WEEK 31: DAY 5

"Hello, my name is _____ and this is Amazing Facts and Crazy Quizzes."

It is always the other person! It may be human nature to blame the other person, but sometimes it is our fault. Think before you accuse others of being mean. Take a good look at what is going on around you. Did you start it? Are you being mean too? Talk to the other person and figure out a way to settle the problem. You started it, now you can stop it like a hero.

Optional ending: "Until next time, this is _____ with Amazing Facts and Crazy Quizzes."

1. Stopbullying.gov | Stop Bullying on the Spot, 2014

A Note to the Student Reader: Amazing Facts is a very important part of the day. Read the text beforehand and make sure you can pronounce each word correctly. Ask an adult for help if you come across a word that is difficult.

Notes:
_____
_____
_____
_____
_____
_____
_____

WEEK 32: DAY 1

"Hello, my name is _____ and this is Amazing Facts and Crazy Quizzes."

Girls Bully Differently: One of the ways Buhle Belle likes to bully is to tell lies about her target. She might tell her victim, "You like so and so," or she might start a rumor about something silly that will embarrass her[1]. If you are a bystander, do not help Buhle Belle taunt her victim by listening or spreading the rumors. Report the student acting like Buhle to a teacher.

Optional ending: "Until next time, this is _____ with Amazing Facts and Crazy Quizzes."

---

1. National Crime Prevention Council, 2015

WEEK 32: DAY 2

"Hello, my name is _____ and this is Amazing Facts and Crazy Quizzes."

Meet the Boomerang-bully. He used to be the victim, but now he is bigger and smarter. He or she now picks on the bully. **A case scenario**: When Sally was in 3rd grade, she was small and shy. Kelly was taller and she liked to push Sally around. One-day Sally realized that Kelly was not very good at math. It was time for her to try out her revenge. She started making fun of Kelly during math time. Kelly started it, but they both need to stop it. Being a boomerang-bully is wrong!

Optional ending: "Until next time, this is _____ with Amazing Facts and Crazy Quizzes."

WEEK 32: DAY 3

"Hello, my name is _____ and this is Amazing Facts and Crazy Quizzes."

Not every bothersome behavior is bullying. Do not call everything bullying. Remember the five rules. Bullies target their victims. Bullying is a constant problem. Bullying involves an imbalance of power in favor of the bully. Bullying is unwanted and meant to do harm. Bullying is not an accident; it is on purpose. **Listen to this case.** Is this person a bully or not? Sam shows up when you are in the hall alone. You do not see him until he starts calling you names. He does this to you every day. (Pause) Is Sam being a bully? The answer is yes.

Optional ending: "Until next time, this is _____ with Amazing Facts and Crazy Quizzes."

WEEK 32: DAY 4

"Hello, my name is _____ and this is Amazing Facts and Crazy Quizzes."

Conflict Resolution: If someone is bothering you, calmly use the strategy TALK. **T**ake control of your emotions- **A**sk them calmly to stop- **L**isten to what they say- **K**eep your promises- Think about this: Why do you need to "Take control of your emotions"? (Pause) The reason is important. Bullies want to make you upset so they can laugh at you. If you stay calm, the bully will not have fun and will probably leave you alone.

Optional ending: "Until next time, this is _____ with Amazing Facts and Crazy Quizzes."

WEEK 32: DAY 5

"Hello, my name is _____ and this is Amazing Facts and Crazy Quizzes."

Students who learn violence tend to join gangs. According to the National Gang Center, gangs have children in them as young as elementary school[1]. A gang is like a bunch of bullies hanging out together. Stay away from gangs. Report them to your school and your parents.

Optional ending: "Until next time, this is _____ with Amazing Facts and Crazy Quizzes."

---

1. Howell, 2010

Yet Another Note to the Student Reader: Sometimes you will come to the word (Pause) in a parenthesis. Do not say the word out loud. It is a direction for you to give a short break before you continue. This will give the audience time to think of the answer before you reveal it.

Notes:
_____
_____
_____
_____
_____
_____
_____

WEEK 33: DAY 1

"Hello, my name is _____ and this is Amazing Facts and Crazy Quizzes."

Conflict Resolution: If someone is bothering you, calmly use the strategy TALK: **T**ake control of your emotions- **A**sk them calmly to stop- **L**isten to what they say (you might be bothering them too)- **K**eep your promises. Think about this: Why do you need to calmly ask them to stop? (Pause) When you are discussing the problem with the other person you need to stay calm and cool. If you yell, this shows that you are upset. Bully Boy loves this reaction. He or she will bully you again. In addition, if you do not stay calm you might look like the bully. Teachers tend to punish the person yelling and not the person bullying.

Optional ending: "Until next time, this is _____ with Amazing Facts and Crazy Quizzes."

WEEK 33: DAY 2

"Hello, my name is _____ and this is Amazing Facts and Crazy Quizzes."

Cyberbullying is when bullying happens online. This happens sometimes during online games. If you run into a bully, report their game-name to the administrator of the server. You could also log off and go to another game site. Elementary students should not use live chat during multiplayer games. Talking to strangers is dangerous. It also opens the door to bullying. Enjoy games created for your age group.

Optional ending: "Until next time, this is _____ with Amazing Facts and Crazy Quizzes."

WEEK 31: DAY 3 (Girls Bully Differently)

"Hello, my name is _____ and this is Amazing Facts and Crazy Quizzes."

One of the ways Buhle Belle likes to bully is to tell lies and spread rumors. She might tell her victim, "You like so and so." She might start a rumor[1]. If you are a bystander, do not help Buhle Belle taunt her victim. Do not listen to the rumors. Do not spread the rumors. Report Buhle to your teacher.

Optional ending: "Until next time, this is _____ with Amazing Facts and Crazy Quizzes."

---

1. National Crime Prevention Council, 2015

WEEK 31: DAY 4

"Hello, my name is _____ and this is Amazing Facts and Crazy Quizzes."

A person's reputation is very important. What will people think when they hear your name? Will they remember you as a troublemaker or a peacekeeper? Will they say you were a bully or a friend?

Optional ending: "Until next time, this is _____ with Amazing Facts and Crazy Quizzes."

WEEK 31: DAY 5

"Hello, my name is _____ and this is Amazing Facts and Crazy Quizzes."

So, you think Joe is the bully? It is very easy for us to assume the other person is the problem. Many people think they are always innocent targets. The amazing fact is, sometimes, YOU are the problem. You are causing them grief in the gym where you are a talented athlete. You trash-talk, brag and put down Joe every time you go to gym class. Now, he is being mean to you in the cafeteria where he has buddies to help. While both of you are wrong, YOU are the bully and he is the boomerang. Stop the cycle of meanness. Talk to the other person, and figure out a way to be friends.

Optional ending: "Until next time, this is _____ with Amazing Facts and Crazy Quizzes."

A Note to the Student Reader: How do you read a web address? It is different from reading a sentence. This is how you say www.stopbulling.gov/kid: you say each "w" like this w.w.w. Stop-bullying (dot) gov (forward slash) kid

Notes:
_____
_____
_____
_____
_____
_____
_____

WEEK 32: DAY 1

"Hello, my name is _____ and this is Amazing Facts and Crazy Quizzes."

Teachers, what do you do if a student tells you that a bully is picking on them? Here are some tips from Stopbullying.gov: Separate the bully and target. Make sure everyone is safe. Ask another adult to help if needed. Report the incident to the administrator in charge of discipline in the school[1].

Optional ending: "Until next time, this is _____ with Amazing Facts and Crazy Quizzes."

---

1. Stopbullying.gov | Stop Bullying on the Spot, 2014

WEEK 32: DAY 2 (Revenge, Getting Even)

"**Hello, my name is _____ and this is Amazing Facts and Crazy Quizzes.**"

The **Boomerang-bully is a target turned revenger.** It happens when the target or victim finds a way to have power over the bully and seeks revenge on them.

A case scenario: When Larry was in 2nd grade he was smaller than most of his peers. Kingston was taller and he liked to call Larry names and make fun of him. During the summer, Larry grew very tall and Kingston remained about the same height. Now Larry is getting revenge for what Kingston did to him by calling him the same names. Kingston started it, but Larry needs to stop it. Stop the cycle of bullying from the inside out. Decide to stop and become a hero not a zero.

Optional ending: "Until next time, this is _____ with Amazing Facts and Crazy Quizzes."

WEEK 32: DAY 3

"**Hello, my name is _____ and this is Amazing Facts and Crazy Quizzes.**"

Not every bothersome behavior is bullying. So remember the five rules. Those who bully target their victims. They are a constant problem. Bullying involves an imbalance of power. Bullying is unwanted and meant to do harm. It is not an accident. It is on purpose.

Optional ending: "Until next time, this is _____ with Amazing Facts and Crazy Quizzes."

WEEK 32: DAY 4

"Hello, my name is _____ and this is Amazing Facts and Crazy Quizzes."

Conflict Resolution: If someone is bothering you, calmly use the strategy TALK. **T** stands for <u>T</u>ake control of your emotions-. **A** stands for <u>A</u>sk them calmly to stop- **L** stands for <u>L</u>isten to what they say (you might be bothering them too)-. **K** stands for <u>K</u>eep your promises. Think about this: Why do you need to "Take control of your emotions"? (Pause) The reason is important: Bullies want to make you upset so they can laugh at you. If you stay calm, the bully will not have fun and will probably leave you alone.

Optional ending: "Until next time, this is _____ with Amazing Facts and Crazy Quizzes."

WEEK 32: DAY 5

"Hello, my name is _____ and this is Amazing Facts and Crazy Quizzes."

A gang is serious trouble. According to the National Gang Center, gangs have children in them as young as elementary school[1]. A gang is an organized group of young criminals. Gangs work together to fight, hurt, rob, and kill. They try to act cool, but they are not. Think of a gang as a bunch of bullies working together to hurt you.

Optional ending: "Until next time, this is _____ with Amazing Facts and Crazy Quizzes."

Write down a hotline you recommend and share it.

---

1. Howell, 2010

Yet Another Note to the Student Reader: Sometimes you will come to the word (Pause) in a parenthesis. Do not say the word out loud. It is a direction for you to give a short break before you continue. This will allow the audience time to think of the answer.

Notes:
_____
_____
_____
_____
_____
_____
_____

WEEK 33: DAY 1

"Hello, my name is _____ and this is Amazing Facts and Crazy Quizzes."

Conflict Resolution: If someone is bothering you, calmly use the strategy TALK: **T**ake control of your emotions- **A**sk them calmly to stop- **L**isten to what they say (you might be bothering them too)- **K**eep your promises. Think about this: Why do you need to "**K**eep your promises"? (Pause) When you are discussing the problem with the other person, you need to listen and figure out what is best for everyone. Listen to this Case Scenario: You ask Bernie to stop kicking your feet. You find out that you are stretching out and your feet are under his desk. To make things better, you agree to keep your feet under your own desk. So keep your promise.

Optional ending: "Until next time, this is _____ with Amazing Facts and Crazy Quizzes."

WEEK 33: DAY 2

"Hello, my name is _____ and this is Amazing Facts and Crazy Quizzes."

Cyberbullying is when bullying happens online. This happens sometimes during online games. If you run into a bully, report their game-name to the admin of the server. You could also log off and go to another game site. Multiplayer games are usually for people seventeen years and older. Do not ruin your childhood by playing adult games on lines. You may have nightmares. You might learn foul language, and other bad habits. Enjoy games created for your age group.

Optional ending: "Until next time, this is _____ with Amazing Facts and Crazy Quizzes."

WEEK 33: DAY 3

"Hello, my name is _____ and this is Amazing Facts and Crazy Quizzes."

People who are friendly and have a good sense of humor tend to be targeted less by bullies. Even when you have to change schools and advance to the next grade, your friends can go with you. Team up this year and be ready for the adventures of next school year.

Optional ending: "Until next time, this is _____ with Amazing Facts and Crazy Quizzes."

WEEK 33: DAY 4

"Hello, my name is _____ and this is Amazing Facts and Crazy Quizzes."

What is the worst thing a teacher could do to a person who chooses to be a bully or Bear? (Pause) The worst thing would be to ignore them and let them get away with their aggression. Research shows that bullies and Bears are more likely to grow up to abuse alcohol. They are also more likely to use illegal drugs, and commit crimes. Those who bully are more likely to spend time in jail[1]. Bad behavior and poor choices will eventually lead to big trouble. If adults do not help students change, their future does not look very good.

Optional ending: "Until next time, this is _____ with Amazing Facts and Crazy Quizzes."

WEEK 33: DAY 5

"Hello, my name is _____ and this is Amazing Facts and Crazy Quizzes."

What do you do if a fellow student tells you that a bully is bothering them? If you are a student, try to be a friend to them. Encourage them to tell a teacher or staff member. Since bullying usually takes place in the halls, playground and cafeteria, ask the target to stick with you and your friends. Bullies do not like a posse of friends.

Optional ending: "Until next time, this is _____ with Amazing Facts and Crazy Quizzes."

---

1. Seely, Tombari, Bennett and Dunkle, 2011

Note to the Student Reader: When you come across ____ spaces, you call them "blank." Example: Bullies (Blank) their victims. After you repeat the question with the "blank," read the sentence with the answer.

Notes:
_____
_____
_____
_____
_____
_____
_____

WEEK 34: DAY 1 (Crazy Quiz # 23)

"Hello, my name is _____ and this is Amazing Facts and Crazy Quizzes."

Know the Usual Suspects! Not all schools talk about Bears, Badgers, Bigfoots, and Bucks, the more you know about the Usual Suspects the more prepared you will be for your new class or new school next year.

Who Am I? I daydream, I bump into things, and I am clumsy. My name is ____? (Pause) The answer is Bernie or Betsy Bigfoot.

Optional ending: "Until next time, this is _____ with Amazing Facts and Crazy Quizzes."

WEEK 34: DAY 2

"Hello, my name is _____ and this is Amazing Facts and Crazy Quizzes."

Being a part of a gang is dangerous business. Research shows there are many risks of being in a gang. These risks include failing grades, poor school attendance, and school dropout[1]. Finishing school will help you be successful in life. Being a part of a gang will help you be a failure.

Optional ending: "Until next time, this is _____ with Amazing Facts and Crazy Quizzes."

WEEK 34: DAY 3 (Crazy Quiz # 24)
"Hello, my name is _____ and this is Amazing Facts and Crazy Quizzes."

Be ready for next year know the Usual Suspects! **Who Am I?** Things are going good until I am stuck in a reading circle at the teacher's table. I will do anything not to read in front of my classmates. I might throw a tantrum or even throw a desk. Who am I? (Pause) The answer is Bingo the Dingo.

Optional ending: "Until next time, this is _____ with Amazing Facts and Crazy Quizzes."

---

1. Howell, 2010

WEEK 34: DAY 4 (Conflict Resolution)

"Hello, my name is _____ and this is Amazing Facts and Crazy Quizzes."

If you use TALK and the person bothering you shows that they are trying to be mean by what they say or react, WALK away immediately. **W**alk do not run- **A**way from the person- **L**ook for a safe place near friends or an adult- **K**eep your cool. If a person is talking mean or arguing, you do not have to listen to them. Staying only gives them more power. Turn around and WALK.

Think about this: "Why do we WALK and not run? (Pause) The answer is important: If you run, the other person may think it is a game and chase you. If you run, they may think you are afraid and an easy target. When you WALK away, you should have your head up, shoulders back and walk with confidence[1].

Optional ending: "Until next time, this is _____ with Amazing Facts and Crazy Quizzes."

WEEK 34: DAY 5 (Crazy Quiz # 25)

"Hello, my name is _____ and this is Amazing Facts and Crazy Quizzes."

Not all schools know about the Usual Suspects! The more you know the more prepared you will be for your new class or new school next year.
Who Am I? I pick, I kick, and I may even lick. I think I am being a friend and we are having a good time playing. Who am I? (Pause) The answer is Billy or Becca Badger.

Optional ending: "Until next time, this is _____ with Amazing Facts and Crazy Quizzes."

1. Beane, 2014

A New Note to the Student Reader: As you read the Amazing Facts and Crazy Quizzes, make sure to respect the punctuation. Periods (.) are like a stop sign. Take a short break at each period. You might take a breath at the period. Keeping the sentences separated by a short break helps keep the meaning clear.

Notes:

_____
_____
_____
_____
_____
_____
_____

WEEK 35: DAY 1 (Rule #1 Review)

"Hello, my name is _____ and this is Amazing Facts and Crazy Quizzes."

If Bullies target their victims, why do bullies pick on that certain person? One reason could be that the target reminds the bully of a person who use to pick on them. Their bad memories pick out the victim. They want revenge on the other person that bullied them. A person they are afraid to face. Do not let your bad feelings make you make bad choices[1]. Bullying is never the right thing to do.

Optional ending: "Until next time, this is _____ with Amazing Facts and Crazy Quizzes."

---

1. McLeod, 2008

WEEK 35: DAY 2 (Rule #2 Review)

"Hello, my name is _____ and this is Amazing Facts and Crazy Quizzes."

Bullying is a constant problem. How do you know you have a bully problem? One way to know is how you react when you see that person. If you will think to yourself, "what will they do to me now?" you probably have a problem. If the bullying has been going on for a long time, talking to an adult for help may be the only way for it to stop.

Optional ending: "Until next time, this is _____ with Amazing Facts and Crazy Quizzes."

WEEK 35: DAY 3 (Rule # 5 Review)

"Hello, my name is _____ and this is Amazing Facts and Crazy Quizzes."

Bullying is not an accident. There are many accidents, however, that may look like bullying. If we pay attention, follow hallway rules like do not run, learn to take turns and practice patience we can stop accidents and help everyone feel safe. Remember, accidents are seldom caused by accident. They are usually caused because someone did not follow the rules or did not pay attention!

Optional ending: "Until next time, this is _____ with Amazing Facts and Crazy Quizzes."

WEEK 35: DAY 4 (Rule # 4 Review)

"Hello, my name is _____ and this is Amazing Facts and Crazy Quizzes."

Bullying is unwanted aggression meant to do harm. When we think of aggression, we think of hitting, kicking, and fighting. You might ask yourself, who would want to be punched or kicked? The amazing fact is there are both boys and girls who like to play rough. It might have started at home with dad or an older sibling roughhousing or play fighting. Students who like to fight are called Bucks in the Usual Suspects. They may be your friend and just want to play. Use TALK-WALK-TELL if you need to.

Optional ending: "Until next time, this is _____ with Amazing Facts and Crazy Quizzes."

WEEK 35: DAY 5 (Rule #3 Review)

"Hello, my name is _____ and this is Amazing Facts and Crazy Quizzes."

Bullying always involves an imbalance of power. The one who bullies thinks he has power. The victim thinks he or she cannot defend himself or herself. The real power the bully has over the victim is not physical, but on the inside. It takes inward courage to report a problem like bullying. This may be the only way the bullying will stop.

Optional ending: "Until next time, this is _____ with Amazing Facts and Crazy Quizzes."

Share your school districts bully hotline:

Record the number here

Yet Another Note to the Student Reader: Sometimes you will come to the word (Pause) in a parenthesis. Do not say the word out loud. It is a direction for you to give a short break before you continue. This will allow the audience time to think of the answer.

Notes:
_____
_____
_____
_____
_____
_____
_____

WEEK 36: DAY 1 (Crazy Quiz # 26)

"Hello, my name is _____ and this is Amazing Facts and Crazy Quizzes."

It is the last week of school, will bullying increase, or decrease? (Pause) It is really up to you and your classmates. By now, the school staff should know who the bullies and Bears are and have them on a behavior plan. How will you act this last week of school? Remember to follow class rules and stay safe. This last week is practice for next year! Will you be a hero or just another kid who has not learned his or her lesson yet?

Optional ending: "Until next time, this is _____ with Amazing Facts and Crazy Quizzes."

WEEK 36: DAY 2

"Hello, my name is _____ and this is Amazing Facts and Crazy Quizzes."

If you are going to a new school next year take the time to meet your new school counselor and the new principals. Ask them if they know about TALK-WALK- TELL or The Usual Suspects. You might need to find them a copy of Amazing Facts and Crazy Quizzes. You can help your new teachers to be up-to-date with bullying. Become your school's bully Czar.

Optional ending: "Until next time, this is _____ with Amazing Facts and Crazy Quizzes."

WEEK 36: DAY 3

"Hello, my name is _____ and this is Amazing Facts and Crazy Quizzes."

Bullies do not take the summer off. Bullying can happen at fun summer spots like the pool, the park, and at summer camp. Stay alert and remember to use TALK, WALK, and TELL. If you need assistance, remember that the lifeguard and camp counselors are there to help.

Optional ending: "Until next time, this is _____ with Amazing Facts and Crazy Quizzes."

WEEK 36: DAY 4

"Hello, my name is _____ and this is Amazing Facts and Crazy Quizzes."

Research shows that many individuals who bully stop for one reason or another[1]. They might be going through a difficult time or things just went wrong somehow. The next time you see that person after the summer break they could act differently toward you. Act friendly toward them. Give them a chance to show how they have changed. Do not remind them of how they acted. They will probably not remember. Some things are best forgotten.

Optional ending: "Until next time, this is _____ with Amazing Facts and Crazy Quizzes."

WEEK 36: DAY 5

"Hello, my name is _____ and this is Amazing Facts and Crazy Quizzes."

Today is your last chance this school year to be a hero. Say you are sorry if you need to. Say thank you to those who helped you along the way. Determine in your heart that next year you will be a leader, not a follower; a helper not a hurter; a buddy and not a bully. Have a great summer.

Optional ending: "Until next time, this is _____ with Amazing Facts and Crazy Quizzes."

Thank you for using Amazing facts and Crazy Quizzes!

1. Dake, Price, Telljohaun, 2003

References:

Anderson, S., & Swiatowy, C. (2008). Bullying Prevention in the Elementary Classroom using Social Skills, ERIC, http://files.eric.ed.gov/fulltext/ED503060.pdf

Beane, Allan L. Ph.D. (2014) Assertiveness https://www.bullyfree.com/free-resources/assertiveness-strategies-for-bullied-students, Retrieved April 11, 2015

Beane, A. (2005). Bullying in American Schools: A Socio-Ecological Perspective on Prevention and Intervention. D. L. Espelage & S. M. Swearer (Eds.). Mawah, NJ: Lawrence Erlbaum Associates, 2003,. *The Journal of Primary Prevention,* 467-468.

Bullying: Facts for Schools and Parents. (2003, October 3). National Center for Education Statistics, Retrieved January 10, 2015, from http://www.nasponline.org/resources/factsheets/bullying_fs.aspx

Cohn, A., & Canter, A. (1999, January 1). Why Do Some Children and Adolescents Become Bullies? Retrieved December 22, 2014, from http://www.nasponline.org/resources/factsheets/bullying_fs.aspx

Dake, J., Price, J., & Telljohann, S. (2003). The Nature and Extent of Bullying at School. *Journal of School Health, 73*(5), 173-180.

Harper, Douglas, 1999, Online Etymology Dictionary. (n.d.). Retrieved December 22, 2014, from http://www.etymonline.com/index.php?term=bully

Eder, D., & Enke, J. (1991). The Structure of Gossip: Opportunities and Constraints on Collective Expression among Adolescents. *American Sociological Review, 54*(4), 494-508.

Elliott, M. (2002). *Bullying: A practical guide to coping for schools* (3rd ed., pp. 8-14). London: Pearson Education [published in association with] Kidscape.

Fagan, A., & Mazerolle, P. (2011). Repeat Offending and Repeat Victimization: Assessing Similarities and Differences In Psychosocial Risk Factors. *Crime & Delinquency, 57*(5), 732-755.

Field, T. (1996). Bully in sight: How to predict, resist, challenge and combat workplace bullying: Overcoming the silence and denial by which abuse thrives. Wantage, England: Success Unlimited.

Georgiou, S., & Stavrinides, P. (2013). Parenting at home and bullying at school. *Social Psychology of Education, 16*(2), 165-179.

Goodreads. (2015, January 1). Eleanor Roosevelt Quotes. Retrieved January 4, 2015, from https://www.goodreads.com/author/quotes/44566.Eleanor_Roosevelt, Grose, F., &

Hoover, J., & Stenhjam, P. (2003). Bullying and Teasing of Youth with Disabilities: Creating Positive School Environments for Effective Inclusion. *Issue Brief, 2*(3). Retrieved from ERIC.

Howell, J. (2010). Gang Prevention: An Overview of Research and Programs. Juvenile Justice Bulletin. Retrieved January 10, 2015, from ERIC.

Juvonen, J., Wang, Y., & Espinoza, G. (2013). Physical Aggression, Spreading of Rumors, and Social Prominence in Early Adolescence: Reciprocal Effects Supporting Gender Similarities. *Journal of Youth and Adolescence, 42*(12), 1801-1810.

Kaiser, B., & Rasminsky, J. (2009). *Challenging behavior in elementary and middle school.* Upper Saddle River, N.J.: Pearson.

Kephart, H. (1915). *Castaways and Crusoes; tales of survivors of ship-wreck in New Zealand, Patagonia, Tobago, Cuba, Magdalen Islands, South Seas and the Crozets,.* New York: Outing Pub.

Lereya, S., Samara, M., & Wolke, D. (2013). Parenting behavior and the risk of becoming a victim and a bully/victim: A meta-analysis study. *Child Abuse & Neglect,* 1091-1108.

Mathews, A. (2007). *Restoring My Soul: A Workbook for Finding and Living the Authentic Self* (p. 329 pages). IUniverse.

McLeod, S. (2009, January 1). Defense Mechanisms | Simply Psychology. Retrieved December 23, 2014, from http://www.simplypsychology.org/defense-mechanisms.html

NEA, How to Identify Bullying. (2015). Retrieved January 2, 2015, from http://www.nea.org/home/53359.htm

National Crime Prevention Council. (2015, January 1). Girls and Bullying. Retrieved January 5, 2015, from http://www.ncpc.org/topics/bullying/girls-and-bullying

Ockerman, M., Mason, E., & Hollenbeck, A. (2012). Integrating RTI with School Counseling Programs: Being a Proactive Professional School Counselor. *Journal of School Counseling, 10*(15), 37-37. Retrieved January 17, 2015, from http://eric.ed.gov/?

Olweus, D. (1978). Aggression in the schools: Bullies and whipping Boys. Oxford, England: Hemisphere.

Olweus, D., & Mortimore, P. (1993). *Bullying at school: What we know and what we can do*. Oxford, England: Blackwell Publishing

Paone, T., & Lepkowski, W. (2007). No Childhood Left Behind: Advocating for the Personal and Social Development of Children. *Journal of School Counseling., 5*(25), 18-18. Retrieved January 17, 2015, from http://eric.ed.gov/?

Peters, M. (2010, October 30). The History of the Word Bully: A Vicious, Cowardly Word with a Long History. Retrieved December 22, 2014, from http://magazine.good.is/articles/the-history-of-the-word-bully

Rigby, Ken. *Bullying in Schools and What to Do about It*. Rev. and Updated. ed. Camberwell, Vic.: ACER, 2007. Print.

Steiger, L. (1987). Participant Workbook. In *Nonviolent crisis intervention: A program focusing on management of disruptive, assaultive, or out-of-control behavior* (p. 13). Brookfield, Wis.: National Crisis Prevention Institute.

Stopbullying.gov | Bystander. (2014). U.S. Department of Health and Human services. Retrieved December 23, 2014, from www.stopbullying.gov/respond/be-more-than-a-bystander/index.html

Stopbullying.gov | Cyberbullying. (2014). U.S. Department of Health and Human services. Retrieved December 23, 2014, from www.stopbullying.gov/cyberbullying/index.html

Stopbullying.gov | Definition. (2014). U.S. Department of Health and Human services. Retrieved December 23, 2014, from www.stopbullying.gov/what-is-bullying/definition/index.html

Stopbullying.gov | How to Talk About bullying. (2014). U.S. Department of Health and Human services. Retrieved December 23, 2014, from www.stopbullying.gov/prevention/talking-about-it/

Stopbullying.gov | Laws. (2014). U.S. Department of Health and Human services. Retrieved December 23, 2014, from www.stopbullying.gov/what-is-bullying/definition/index.html

Stopbullying.gov | Risk Factors. (2014). U.S. Department of Health and Human services. Retrieved December 23, 2014, from www.stopbullying.gov/at-risk/factors/index.html#atrisk

Stopbullying.gov | Stop Bullying on the Spot. (2014). U.S. Department of Health and Human services. Retrieved December 23, 2014, from www.stopbullying.gov/respond/on-the-spot/index.html

Stopbullying.gov | Support the Kids Involved. (2014). U.S. Department of Health and Human services. Retrieved December 23, 2014, from www.stopbullying.gov/respond/support-kids-involved/

Stopbullying.gov | The Roles Kids Play. (2014). U.S. Department of Health and Human services. Retrieved December 23, 2014, from www.stopbullying.gov/what-is-bullying/roles-kids-play

Stopbullying.gov | What You Can Do. (2014). U.S. Department of Health and Human services. Retrieved December 23, 2014, from www.stopbullying.gov/kids/what-you-can-do/

Tripp, R. (1970). *The international thesaurus of quotations*. New York: Crowell.

Understanding School Violence: Fact Sheet. (2008, January 17). Retrieved January 17, 2015,
from http://www.cdc.gov/violenceprevention/pdf/school_violence_fact_sheet-a.pdf

Other Books by the Author

This is a fun book for pre-k and kinder children. Lisa learns about reading and confidence beneath her reading tree. Professionals can also use the illustrations to talk to elementary aged students about illness in the family. A portion of profits are donated to the National Cancer Society through Legacy Demolay- a Texas chapter of Demolay International.

Use the QR code to purchase the book on Amazon.com

The World's Strongest Human is a true story about a foster child who grew up to be a superhero. It is an inspirational tale about professional wrestler Bobby LaGree who won a spot in Ripley's Believe it or Not as the only person to ever move 63,000 pounds with his bare hands.

The book is written so both children and adults can enjoy it. Each chapter heading highlights the trait that was demonstrated in the life of Mr. LaGree. School Counselor, David D. Dye narrates the story and gives it a unique flair that will make it an instant classic.

Use the QR code to purchase the book on Amazon.com

The Usual Suspects ID Cards provides an easy way to identify behaviors. The free app works on iPad and on android phones and tablets. Available on iTunes, Google Play and other online app stores.

Lilly's New School was written by JeAuana Evans when she was a third grade student at Mr. Dye's School. Illustrator Jon Dye provided the art work for free and all proceeds go to the young author through her grandparent's account.

Follow the adventure of Lilly as she faces off with Buhle Belle at her new school. You will be surprised how the young author depicts the events and solution.

 Use the QR code to purchase the book on Amazon.com

 Like us on Facebook: Beneath the Reading Tree

 Like us on Facebook: The World's Strongest Human

 Like us on Facebook: Character Academy
(Amazing Facts and Crazy Quizzes and the Usual Suspects)

www.ingramcontent.com/pod-product-compliance
Lightning Source LLC
Chambersburg PA
CBHW050644160426
43194CB00010B/1808